The Bird Seeker's Guide

THE
BIRD SEEKER'S
GUIDE

John Gooders

ANDRE DEUTSCH

First published 1980 by
André Deutsch Limited
105 Great Russell Street London WC1

Copyright © 1981 by John Gooders

Filmset by Servis Filmsetting Limited, Manchester

Printed in Great Britain by
Ebenezer Baylis and Son Limited
The Trinity Press, Worcester, and London

Hardback ISBN 0 233 97297 8
Paperback ISBN 0 233 97380 X

CONTENTS

ILLUSTRATIONS

INTRODUCTION

'Where shall I go?' takes second place only to 'What bird is that?' in the bird-watching beginner's list of most useful phrases, even though in some ways it has an obvious priority. After a while (the exact time depends on the dosage of bird-watching) 'What?' becomes less frequently used as expertise is gained and it is gradually realised that all birds can be identified given time and sufficiently good views. It would not, at that point, seem unreasonable to believe that the 'Where?' element would also decline. In my experience it does not. Soon 'Where?' becomes the only important question, far outweighing the 'What?' of the tyro. Yet this simple 'Where?' question works at a variety of different levels. The watcher sitting in the shore hide at Minsmere asks, 'Where is the dowitcher?' Chatting to others along the East Bank at Cley he asks, 'Where did you see that yellow-browed warbler?' In the evening over a pint in The Bell, Walberswick, the conversation turns to real problems and a 'Where did he say the red-flanked bluetail was nesting?' while eventually the need is for 'Where should I go in Nepal for ibisbill?', or something equally obscure.

In an effort to solve some of these problems I wrote *Where to Watch Birds* and *Where to Watch Birds in Europe*. Both books picked out the very best areas for watching birds in Britain and Europe respectively, but they did not say where to find the particular birds that the bird-watcher might be anxious to see. There thus arose in my mind the need for a guide that reversed the process, that instead of starting with the locations started with the birds themselves. This concept was succintly encapsulated by my publisher Piers Burnett as a 'mirror' of *Where to Watch Birds*. So *The Bird Seeker's Guide* was born, though it was my son Timothy who eventually came up with the title. This seems an appropriate place to express my thanks to both.

There are, of course, obvious problems in dealing with bird-seeking this way around. A locality, even a good one, may have a list of perhaps a hundred species that occur regularly; a bird may occur in virtually every village in Britain and number perhaps seven or eight million pairs. Clearly it is not possible to list every location for every bird, especially if the bird is numerous. However, it is also then quite unnecessary to list every, or even any, location for birds that are so widespread that even the most disinterested could not ignore them. But herein lies yet another catch. For while it is impossible to list all the places where starlings, for instance, can be found it is equally impossible to list any of the traditional sites where peregrine, golden eagle or red kite nest.

It always comes as a total surprise to American birders, for thus they are called west of the Atlantic, that we in Europe are unable to publish exactly how to get to see so many of our birds. American guides are full of '. . . take a left, then a right through the wicket gate and watch out for Louisiana's only breeding bald eagles in a belt of tall trees . . .' Such instructions are unthinkable over here because of the extraordinary tenacity of illegal egg collectors. The activities of these strange, child-like hoarders of empty shells preclude the ordinary bird-watcher from being fully and openly informed of the whereabouts of a considerable number of species that breed regularly in Britain. While this does not prevent any keen bird-watcher from infiltrating the ornitho-grapevine and finding the precise hedgerow in which to search for a marsh warbler, it does create difficulties for the more casual watchers who form the backbone of our bird clubs and societies.

Today, however, another menace threatens to cut back even further on publishable information – the ornitho-vandal. Although they are often labelled as 'young long-hairs' my experience tells me that they come from all age groups, all classes, all parts of the country, and are to be characterized not in terms of their appearance but solely by their behaviour. I once had the good fortune to discover a sizeable group of breeding spotted crakes at an old-fashioned sewage farm. Their 'quip-quip-quip' calls echoed over the flooded grass fields and I was content to have found the birds and let them be. I made, however, the cardinal mistake of informing an officer of the local natural history society and was staggered to find several dozen watchers present the following evening. Despite its being July and the middle of the breeding season, some were tramping across the fields to flush the birds, for a 'tick' demands a sighting.

Personally I'm happy to have 'observed' the bird – and that includes by sound alone if the species is one of the ultra-skulking type. Such stupidity sows the seeds of its own destruction, and it is no wonder that so many bird-watchers keep their local rare breeding (and non-breeding) birds very much to themselves. I am not suggesting for one minute that I am in favour of such mystery, only that it is understandable in the face of a few hooligans who care more for their own pleasures than for the safety of the birds they seek to watch.

Fortunately, as the number of bird-watchers has grown phenomenally over the last twenty years or so, so too has the membership of the various conservation bodies. The Royal Society for the Protection of Birds (RSPB) is now a major voice for conservation in Britain and the owner/leasee of some of the best bird-watching areas in the country. Thus the growing army of bird-watchers is better catered for than ever and, because they live on well-protected reserves, the whereabouts of more rare birds can be made public. Only a few years ago it would have been unthinkable to publish the exact whereabouts of birds as diverse as ospreys, black-tailed godwits and Savi's warblers. Of course, in order to be able to show members unusual birds, the Society has to exercise a considerable amount of control. As a result permits, hides and all the other paraphernalia of organized conservation have become part of our everyday birding experience. Where once a walk along a marshland wall would send birds scurrying over the water or towering into the sky, now carefully sited hides and screens enable birds to be watched undisturbed. There can be no doubt that the extraordinary increase in the number of watchers has made such an approach essential. However, that does not mean that one cannot experience a tinge of regret at the loss of much of the wildness which was formerly such an element in our bird-watching. Anyone who has yet to experience this mass style bird-watching should take a trip to one of the double decker hides that now fringe some of our best marshes.

Another aspect of this increase in the bird-watcher population has been the unprecedented growth of hostility of landowners. 'Keep Out' notices addressed specifically to bird-watchers are to be seen about the birding hot spots, where there were none twenty years ago. The law of trespass is a strange animal that I do not pretend to understand, but bird-watchers who trample over crops, break down fences, leave gates open or interfere in one way or another with the work of farmers are doing the average bird-watcher no good at all. Ultimately, of course, farmers may decide they would be better off without the birds and may take steps to dissuade them from using their land.

The increase in bird-watcher numbers thus has advantages and disadvantages. We may be banned from certain areas while, at the same

time, the organizations to which we belong are opening up new areas
for our enjoyment. It is this latter aspect, the increasingly successful
protection of certain species, that has enabled this book to be written.
Without reserves the whereabouts of many of the most interesting of
British birds could not be published.

Though the main body of the text deals with all of the birds that are
regularly seen in Britain, there are also a remarkably large number of
species that have occurred on so few occasions as to merit the label
'rarity'. The reasons for such an extraordinary list are not difficult to
find. Britain is an offshore island with a huge coastline. To the east lies
Eurasia, one of the world's great land masses from which huge
numbers of birds flee every autumn and to which they return every
spring. To the west is the North Atlantic with only Ireland between us
and the great landmass of North America. Birds that migrate in and out
of that continent regularly take short cuts over the seas and the
prevailing westerly winds sometimes blow them well off course to
their first landfall in Britain and Ireland. In the south is the Mediterranean and the continent of Africa, winter home to millions of
European birds. In spring they fly northwards and many birds of
southern Europe make mistakes and over-fly to reach our shores – a
phenomenon aptly called 'overshooting'. Finally, to the north there is
the huge hostile Arctic Ocean which is so rich that it virtually teems
with seabirds. Some regularly come to our shores, whereas others are
only the rarest of vagrants; among them are some of the most sought
after of British birds.

Being an offshore island Britain has a smaller variety of breeding
birds than the adjacent parts of the continent, but a larger variety than
Ireland, which is even more offshore! But for the same reasons it has a
larger percentage of irregular and vagrant visitors. It is this group
above all others that makes Britain such an exciting place to watch
birds. One literally does not know what will turn up next. Many of
these 'interesting' birds are detailed in the main text and, while they
are liable to appear anywhere, the records show that they turn up in
some spots again and again. Others occur so infrequently that they are
relegated to a separate section on rarities that deals with them more
briefly.

The species text is the guts of this book. It deals with each species
that occurs with any degree of regularity and should enable the keen
bird-watcher to find over two hundred species in a year without too
much trouble. The text is designed to help locate birds and concentrates

on known spots where birds can be found. It is not intended to list every place, only those that are regular and safe. It is not an identification manual, though useful notes are given, but essentially a guide for those seeking to find a particular species. Along the way many other birds will be found, for that is one of the joys of bird-watching.

Throughout the book names of places have been used without recourse to geographical location descriptions. Thus Minsmere is only a small Suffolk coastal marsh on the map and is virtually unknown outside the bird world. Leigh, Radipole, Marazion, Ythan, Rothiemurchus, Farlington, Skokholm – all are familiar enough to the bird-watcher, but totally foreign to both beginner and layman. A gazetteer of places mentioned in the main text is included for reference. Simply look up the bird you want to see and then check the places listed in the gazetteer to see which is nearest.

Some places, however, are mentioned so often that they clearly have either a unique appeal to birds, to bird-watchers, or to both. Some of these are the 'hot spots'; places where watchers congregate in numbers in their efforts to see more birds. Without exception these are migration watch points and are most frequented and most exciting in autumn from August to October. This is the peak time for watching birds in Britain, when every day is exciting, when every sweep with the binoculars may produce the great rarity. Though all of these 'hot spots' are detailed in *Where to Watch Birds**, for the sake of completeness a selection is also given here.

One of the most important tools of any bird-watcher is a reasonable understanding of avian ecology – which is only another way of saying how a bird fits into its background. It is as essential to know that Brent geese are marine as it is that bearded tits are confined to reed beds. Without that knowledge neither species will be found. Much of this boils down to a knowledge of bird habitats and these are detailed for each species. They are of the utmost importance to the bird-seeker and are the subject of a separate chapter.

Throughout this book references are made to organizations such as clubs and societies. It is well known that if two bird-watchers meet they will form a club, and that if three meet they will elect a committee. However, some organizations are essential and membership of them will enable the bird-watcher to improve his knowledge of birds, and

*André Deutsch, 1967.

where to find them, out of all proportion to the fees involved. It is, in my view, inconceivable that one could watch birds in Britain without belonging to the RSPB. Not only is it a good cause, but its activities seem virtually designed to bring bird-watchers of all ages together.

The hoary old subject of the names and sequence of our birds is too lengthy a one for discussion here. I have argued ceaselessly the advantages of a fixed list of English names for all the birds of the world, which would then be used universally. Such a list seems as far away as ever. British insularity is now so well established that foreigners no longer find it vaguely amusing, but increasingly find it positively irritating. Thus robin, swallow, blackbird, dipper, redstart, jay, starling, wheatear and many more besides are names applied not only to a particular British bird but also to groups (often quite large) of species. It has thus been a great temptation to produce the Gooders' List, but a temptation I have put firmly aside. Instead I have followed the order and names adopted by *The 'British Birds' List of Birds of the Western Palearctic* which, compiled by a committee, has all the faults that such bodies are prone to and an inevitable conservatism. In sheer desperation I have added a few vernaculars of my own within the text. Nevertheless all bird-watchers should ensure themselves of an adequate supply of these handy little check-lists.

Finally, and for an introduction this is already far too long, I must thank some of the people who have made this book possible. I have already mentioned Piers Burnett of André Deutsch; but every author needs a good publisher, and Piers is a good publisher. About Hazel Cooper, who turns scribble into typescript, I am running out of things to say. With this book I have tested her loyalty to the limit, but she has still produced an excellent job. To those friends and companions who have suffered along with the writing of this guide, my thanks for their continued indulgence.

John Gooders, *Oxford 1980.*

SEASONS

The idea of there being four seasons – spring, summer, autumn, winter – is as false for the bird-watcher as it is for the farmer, fisherman, forester or general countryman. Birds appear and disappear, court and nest, feed and die in an extraordinary range of different patterns. The late winter, for instance, is the period of starvation for woodpigeons, the date of arrival for wild geese, and the breeding season for crossbills. 'Autumn' migration may start as early as June for lapwings, whereas shorelarks may not arrive until late October. Birds are moving, living, breeding, migrating throughout the year and only July is noted for its lack of really positive bird action. By then most species have bred and raised their young, though some of the pigeons and doves are exceptions to this as to many other rules. They have finished singing. Many are in moult or busily feeding to build up their reserves prior to migration. It is a period of considerable abundance in the countryside and birds take advantage of the fact to get through these vital functions in a predominantly secretive way.

But even dull old July is not without its attractions. Young birds, birds that have just left the nest, start to wander and there is a small flush of departing warblers to be seen on the south coast at places such as Dungeness, and in the London parks. It is not much compared with what will follow, but it can be detected. Lapwings make those westerly summer movements through the country, but lapwings seem always to be moving somewhere, so no one is really likely to get excited about them. Other waders may prove more of an attraction with some of the birds of arctic Europe returning from breeding in the full resplendence of their nuptial plumage. From mid-July into early August is the classic period for the beautiful, black-plumaged spotted redshanks that have left the taiga zone without moulting. Later in the season they arrive in more nondescript garb. A russet-coloured sanderling may have the inexperienced guessing if it feeds on a marsh instead of running about at the tide edge, but a fine 'red' curlew sandpiper or knot will simply prove a wonder and delight. So even July has its attractions.

Bird calendars then, are not easily divided into distinct seasons characterized by a particular activity. Various species, even populations, do different things at different times. There are, however, times or seasons when the majority of species are involved in a particular function.

From December through to February most species face their hardest time of the year. Winter snow covers the ground and prevents ground feeders from getting at their food. Hard frosts prevent other ground feeders from functioning and may initiate hard weather movements towards more gentle climes. Those same frosts may freeze up open water sending duck slipping comically over the ice on our park ponds as they rush for the bread and other scraps of food brought by kindly non-birders. Out on the marshes it is a tougher story for our wildfowl. Occasionally things get so desperate that they will go to any length for food and wildfowlers impose a voluntary ban on shooting them.

During these same months other species are busily establishing and defending their territories while some, like the crossbill for example, are actually getting on with the serious business of nesting. It has always seemed strange to me that egg collectors have invariably defended their perverted passion by stating that most birds will lay a replacement clutch for the one that they have stolen. In doing so they take no account of the fact that birds have evolved an egg-laying season that suits them and which is ideally adapted to maintaining their population. To interfere in such a process must inevitably lessen the chances of a bird's being able to successfully rear a family. Species such as the crossbill lay their eggs in the heart of winter for very good reasons.

However, while there are exceptions to every generalization, some clear patterns do emerge. The bird calendar in Britain finds an easy starting point in mid-March when several of our resident birds are settling down to breed. Mistle thrushes and blackbirds often build nests at this time, hiding them among ivy or some other evergreen or, in the case of the mistle thrush, in the major fork of an otherwise bare tree. At the same time the winter visitors, the wildfowl, redwings and fieldfares are preparing to depart northwards, though inclement weather at this time will throw all systems into reverse. A trickle of early summer visitors may be detected in the south with early chiffchaffs and wheatears bringing a touch of summer to what is often still an inhospitable scene.

Within a few brief weeks all has changed. Mid-April sees most of the winter visitors heading northwards on their way towards breeding grounds that remain in the grip of ice and snow. Resident birds such as robins, dunnocks and song thrushes are getting down to breeding. And the summer visitors begin to pour in. Swallows spread through the country with amazing swiftness, chiffchaffs are everywhere, and there are sizeable arrivals of willow warblers. April remains, however, a month of transition, for though there are comparatively few species of summer migrants that wait until May before they put in a first appearance, the mass arrival of most migrant species does not occur until that month.

May is superb for all bird-watchers except the totally dedicated life lister. For him or her only the scattering of 'overshooting' summer migrants, that is, birds that migrate northwards to southern Europe, but sometimes 'overshoot' to Britain, offer any chance of a new bird for the life list. Meanwhile we more easily satisfied souls have an enormous bonanza establishing contact with all the birds that we have not seen since last year. These include small warblers, the hirundines (swallows and martins), swifts, the cuckoo, waders such as the little ringed plover and common sandpiper and birds as diverse as yellow wagtails and common terns. Quite suddenly the whole countryside seems alive with birds most of which are singing from our hedgerows, reed beds and woods. It is a time of splendid birding to be enjoyed year after year.

At the same time there are many species that, having wintered to the south, are passing through on their way farther north. Waders in particular are often abundant and sometimes spectacularly garbed in full breeding dress. Unlike in autumn, their passage is often swift and they will move on within a few days of their arrival. However, their places may be taken by those of the same or other species so that a well-sited marsh may produce northern waders throughout the month.

Finally by mid- or late May almost all summer visitors are present, the songsters are singing and therefore easy to locate, and there is still a goodly number of passage migrants on the marshes. This is the optimum time for the 'Big Day' – an attempt to see as many species as possible within twenty-four hours. The actual record is 133 species by two observers in a single day. The important elements are a wide variety of habitats within a comparatively small geographical area so that species typical of each can be ticked off with a fair amount of confidence. A good coastal wader marsh where sandpipers can be observed with ease; the coast for terns, gulls and more waders; and a good knowledge of the nesting sites of birds such as owls and nightjars which may be visited after dark when they remain the only possibilities while other birds are asleep. Some of these may have already been picked up earlier in the day before dawn. Clearly there is one other essential ingredient – the stamina of the observers. Unfortunately this book can offer little help on that score, though the unwritten laws of the game do not apparently preclude the use of helpers in finding birds so that they can more easily be located by the Big Day lister himself.

By June all the summer migrants are in and all the winter visitors have gone. A few late birds of passage may still put in an appearance including some high arctic waders, eastern species such as red-footed falcons and the odd late 'overshooter' such as a roller.

Otherwise June is a month for breeding birds and the enthusiast will be busily searching out the rare breeders as he does the rare migrants later in the year. Fieldfare and redwing in the north, serin and golden oriole in the south, roseate tern, ruff, black-tailed godwit, snow bunting, goshawk, Montagu's harrier, hobby and many others are best searched for at this time. For the bird photographer this is the height of the season when all hides are in use and only the shortage of days prevents even more work being achieved.

The following month, July, is a considerable contrast though, as already explained, it is not without its interest. Generally birds are quiet and there is a lull before the excitements of the autumn begin in August.

It cannot really be either the school holidays or the holiday season itself that makes August such an exciting month, though for many bird-watchers it does offer the year's most intensive period actually in the field. The departure of summer visitors begins to get under way and, though no single species cannot still be found in September, many 'last' records for the individual watcher will occur towards the end of August. However, August is primarily a month when waders from the arctic flood southwards through our marshes and when 'falls' of migrants may include a scattering of the less usual birds that seldom occur at any other time of the year. Rare birds may be more numerous in September and rarer in October, but August is the month for real numbers of migrants. Dunlins, frequently associated with the scarcer little stints and curlew sandpipers, are building up in numbers. Wood sandpipers, green sandpipers and greenshanks can be found along the dykes and marshes. Spotted redshanks in 'black' plumage, knot in 'red', even ruffs with what remains of their nuptial finery can all be seen. Terns flood along the coasts and every marsh and reservoir worth its salt is a transient home to black terns and common sandpipers. Little gulls are often numerous and this is almost the only time of the year that the observer is in with a real chance of seeing this diminutive species in Britain. The first trans-Atlantic vagrants of the year will occur, usually pectoral sandpipers, but some other waders as well. With so many birds on the move mix-ups and accidents are bound to occur.

September is the transitional month and similar to May in the wealth of species that can be found. There are, however, two major differences. Firstly, hardly any birds are singing and to identify a 'little brown job' (LBJ) deep inside a bush requires either an immense amount of patience, or an intimate knowledge of the odd calls that every species is capable of producing. Secondly, most of the waders are happy to proceed at a much more leisurely pace and indeed stay off-passage at particularly suitable places for weeks at a time. Thus small birds are more difficult to locate and waders much easier.

Not surprisingly rare waders are *the* birds of the month and a white-rumped sandpiper, for instance, may be seen by upwards of a thousand enthusiasts in a week. It is September during which the ornitho-grapevine – a sort of rarities hotline – really begins to hum, and during which sudden illnesses prevent rarity hunters from attending work, and when those odd days' leave kept in reserve are frittered away on twitch after twitch.

This is the month when every 'hot spot' is manned daily, and each spot has its own fans. For some, September away from Fair Isle is unthinkable, whereas others like to keep all their options open and stay on the mainland ready to strike off in any direction. Migrant falls will include willow warblers, pied flycatchers, redstarts and the occasional wryneck or bluethroat. Rarities such as greenish and arctic warblers, red-breasted flycatchers and Richard's pipits will occur and American waders will become almost regular in some places. Among these diverse elements a strange new bird to Britain will occur, or at least be claimed; though it is surprising how many such reports just seem to evaporate when an actual claim has to be made.

By the end of September things have calmed down considerably. The masses of birds have disappeared and arrivals tend to be lighter with only the occasional heavy fall. October has a different air, autumn is coming and birds of a different degree of rarity can be expected. Now there is a real chance of a major rarity occurring and the stalwarts are all off to the south-west in the hope of an American passerine or two to add to their lists and possibly to that of Britain.

Extremely rare eastern birds such as Radde's and Pallas's warblers may appear – it is a poor autumn when there are none – as well as something quite unexpected. It is a time when no bird should be ignored, when every 'cheep' from inside a bush may prove to be *the* bird.

It is also a time to watch for the arrival of winter visitors, for though the occasional redwing, fieldfare and brambling have turned up in September, the main arrivals of these species occur in October. Wildfowl too begin to flood in and the number of ducks on reservoirs begins to build up to its winter peak. Geese are flooding into the north and Loch Leven is a splendid place to be towards the end of the month. Further south, on the east coast, Bewick's swans are dropping into the marshes and the odd hen harrier may be seen quartering the reed beds or beating over a coastal heath. Merlins may be in evidence when starling flocks come to roost among the reeds and huge movements of these birds together with vast flocks of finches may be seen soon after dawn, and occasionally all day long. These movements are best seen along the coast or over a large urban area where they are more obvious, but they occur throughout the country.

Then comes November and the last of the big migrations with thousands of thrushes entering the country along with large numbers of different species of wildfowl. It is also the season of storms and gales and these too, though not good for the birds themselves, are not to be ignored by bird-watchers. Unusual seabirds, such as little auks, are regularly driven inshore to find shelter on some coastal lagoon, or even inland reservoir or pond. True birds of the north like glaucous gulls may turn up in all sorts of different places, though coastal rubbish dumps and gull roosts are the favoured hunting grounds.

Slowly, through the month, winter takes a grip and things begin to settle down. By December most of our winter visitors are on station and movements are confined to nomadic wanderings in search of food, and hard weather movements by those particularly sensitive feeders – the lapwings. By the New Year most bird-watching consists of visiting the regular haunts of geese in the search for the odd rare bird that has become mixed up with the flocks. A red-breasted goose at Slimbridge, a snow goose in Scotland, a lesser white-front among the bean geese. Rough-legged buzzards and hen harriers can be found on the east coast, a peregrine at Slimbridge, huge, even monumental, wader flocks on the Ribble and at Morecambe Bay. And so it continues through February until before long it is March again and the first wheatear can be spotted along the south coast taking us full circle.

Each season then has its attractions and each is full of variety. At all times of the year there is a choice of venue, but the essential thing is to know not only what to look for, but when and where to look for it.

HABITATS

Birds are the most mobile of all animals. In a few minutes they can travel over a mile and move from one area to another that is completely different. Many make long seasonal journeys that take them from one part of the world to another, and even the most sedentary of species frequently make movements that are geared to feeding, courting, roosting and so on. Yet each species has its own particular niche, a habitat that is very much its own and in which it finds the ideal conditions for its existence. It is thus as foolhardy to look for a puffin in an oak wood as it is to expect to see a great spotted woodpecker clinging to a seacliff. Birds are creatures of habitat, as well as habit, and a knowledge of the preferred life-zones of every species is not only in itself interesting, but is also essential to the bird seeker.

The apparent problem of reconciling the notions of birds being highly mobile and at the same time confined to a particular habitat is overcome by the air. Air space, save for a handful of almost totally aerial species, can be regarded as neutral ground – an element to be passed through as a species leaves one piece of habitat on its way to another similar piece. The great spotted woodpecker may fly past my window overlooking a meadow, but it is on its way from one tree to another. I should be very surprised if it landed and started to feed on the ground. Trees are to woodpeckers what the sea is to puffins.

Of course, the vagaries of migration often bring birds into quite unsuitable areas where they have little choice but to land. At such times quite extraordinary occurences may be spotted – a puffin standing at a bus queue in The Strand for example. Yet even under such duress birds seek out the nearest equivalent of their natural surroundings. A cream-coloured courser finds a sandy beach as near as it can get to its natural desert environment. A stone-curlew confronted with the huge urban sprawl of London seeks out a children's sand pit in Kilburn. The storm-bound little auk heads for the nearest large reservoir. So even *in extremis* birds will attempt to find areas that most closely resemble their natural niche.

Not all birds, however, are as confined as the great spotted woodpecker and even that bird will leave the woods to scour a hedgerow, a suburban garden, or even visit a bird table. Species such as the starling are immensely successful simply by virtue of their adaptability. Starlings can be found in cities feeding among the town pigeons, on wild coastal marshes, in woods occupying old woodpecker holes, on desolate tree-less islands and among the gulls and auks on sea-swept cliffs. House sparrows are numerous and widespread too, but they are confined by their inability to live very far from man. In the mountains of Norway, for instance, summer dwellings have a resident pair of white wagtails instead of house sparrows because the latter cannot survive the winter absence of people.

Nature, and that includes the way in which birds are related to their habitats, is never static. Things change. In Britain reed buntings have spread away from purely aquatic habitats to occupy areas that, only a few years ago, would have seemed quite unsuitable. They can now be found even in suburban gardens, though the latter is an artificial habitat that has forced a good number of species to change the way in which they live.

Great tits, blue tits, robins, blackbirds, all are essentially woodland birds that have taken advantage of the opportunities offered by gardens. The feeders and nest boxes are only the most obvious outward signs of what is an extremely rich habitat created quite artificially within the last hundred years or so. It is really not at all surprising that birds have been so quick to take advantage of their bountifulness. This dynamic is, of course, very interesting to students of ecology, but it does not mean that birds are any the less creatures of habit. A sound knowledge of what birds are found where remains an essential tool to every bird-watcher.

In this chapter habitats will be outlined in a classification loosely based on that proposed by W.B. Yapp, but adapted and simplified for our practical needs. The whole landscape is broken down into types based on a series of divisions and sub-divisions. The typical species of each habitat are given together with, where appropriate, some idea of abundance. In the sections on woodlands I am particularly indebted to W.B. Yapp whose *Birds and Woods** I have always found so useful and absorbing.

---

*Birds and Woods, W.B. Yapp, OUP © 1962

Woodland

Woods can be regarded as falling into three major types: deciduous, coniferous and mixed. The birds of each type naturally overlap to a certain extent, but this overlap is not complete and some species are positively confined to one type or the other. Even within the category of deciduous woodland there are distinct differences between, say, oak woods and beech woods. And even with oak woods there are differences between the bird populations of sessile and pedunculate oaks. Similar distinctions can be drawn between coniferous woods.

Oak Woods

These woods are generally found in southern and western Britain. Pedunculate oak is the common species in the woods of southern England and is characterized by a canopy that is insufficient to prevent the growth of a strong shrub layer, often of hazel. Birds of great variety find their ideal niche here, including, roughly in order of abundance: chaffinch, willow warbler, robin, wren, blackbird, blue tit and great tit, followed by jay, chiffchaff, redstart, song thrush, mistle thrush and cuckoo. Other species present include tree pipit, blackcap, garden warbler, woodpigeon and jackdaw, and lesser numbers of great spotted woodpecker, carrion crow and sparrowhawk.

Sessile oaks are typically found in the west, on the hillsides of the Welsh valleys for example. They are generally damp and the underlying geology prevents the growth of a strong layer of shrubs. The trees are often covered with moss and lichens. Once again the chaffinch is the dominant species and is, if anything, even more abundant. Species in order of abundance include: chaffinch, wood warbler, pied flycatcher, robin, willow warbler, wren, tree pipit, coal tit, redstart, woodpigeon, carrion crow, great tit and blackbird, together with blue tit and buzzard. The differences are quite clear with wood warbler and pied flycatcher taking prominent places in sessile woods while being totally absent from pedunculate woods.

Birch Woods

Birches grow in a variety of different areas and are invariably early colonizers of heath and swamp. They gradually give way to other deciduous species, especially oak. Bird-watchers often find these open woods more satisfying than a climax woodland, probably because birds are easier to see. The chaffinch is still dominant, but the willow warbler finds such woods ideal and may be almost equally as numerous. Species: chaffinch, willow warbler, tree pipit, robin, wren, pied flycatcher, carrion crow, yellowhammer, blue tit, wood warbler, redstart, spotted flycatcher. The presence of the pied flycatcher depends on whether or not the birch wood is located in the north and west of Britain. Such woods in southern England do not hold this species, indicating that a knowledge of habitats must be tempered by a knowledge of distribution. In Scottish birch woods, for example, the willow warbler is three times as numerous as the chaffinch which is in turn almost equalled by the number of tree pipits.

Ash Woods

Pure ash woodland is far from common in Britain yet it is a distinct form of wood and, where it occurs, has an interesting avifauna. Ash often grows over rocky soils and its bird population is more or less intermediate between that of pedunculate and sessile oak woods. Species: willow warbler, chaffinch, redstart, woodpigeon, wren, tree pipit, great tit, blackbird, robin, blue tit, carrion crow, yellowhammer, marsh tit and song thrush. The relative abundance of the redstart is doubtless due to the presence of a large quantity of holes suitable for nesting.

Beech Woods

Beeches are typical of the rolling hilly districts of southern England and their bird population reflects this distinct bias. They differ from the oakwoods that often occur nearby in having a very dense canopy that usually inhibits the growth of a strong shrub layer. Nevertheless their bird population shows some remarkable similarities. Species: chaffinch, great tit, blackbird, wren, willow warbler, woodpigeon, robin, blue tit, chiffchaff, blackcap, jay, nuthatch, song thrush. The wood warbler, so often thought of as such a typical member of the beech wood community, is, in fact, far more abundant in sessile oakwoods.

Winter

In winter many species are absent and their places taken by others. Willow warblers, chiffchaffs, blackcaps, garden warblers, tree pipits and pied flycatchers are all summer visitors, all but a handful of which leave the country completely between October and March. Chaffinches remain in large numbers and are joined, particularly in beech woods, by immigrant bramblings to flock together feeding on the fallen beech-mast. Tits form mixed flocks, often accompanied by treecreepers, nuthatches and other species that roam nomadically through the woods. At such times many woods may seem almost devoid of bird life only to come alive as a flock moves through.

Pine Woods

The native Scot's pine can be found in various parts of Britain where it has been introduced. Areas such as the Brecks of East Anglia were planted in the eighteenth and nineteenth centuries, but many more areas have been planted since. Pure natural pine woods exist only in a few areas of the Scottish Highlands and are even then only a semblance of their former selves. They are, however, quite distinct and have a bird population that differs in many ways from that of other British woods. Special birds include crested tit, crossbill and capercaillie, but these species are far from numerous. Species typical of such pine forests in order of abundance are: chaffinch, willow warbler, coal tit, tree pipit, redstart, meadow pipit, goldcrest, song thrush, cuckoo, carrion crow, robin, crested tit and wren.

Exotic Woods

The latter part of last century and the present century has seen an ever-increasing programme of planting foreign conifers throughout Britain. Usually they are planted in solid blocks and form an ugly addition to our landscape. However, recent plantings have taken more account of non-forestry needs and plantations are now more generally merged into the landscape by being irregularly shaped and masked with plantings of birch and other deciduous species. Even so a twenty-five year old plantation is a pretty dismal place. Trees are all of the same size, the same distance apart and uniformly straight and towering. At maturity they are felled *en bloc* and the process started over again. The most commonly planted species are the sitka and Norwegian spruces, the European and Japanese larches, the lodge-pole pine, Douglas fir and Corsican pine.

Being artificially planted these woods pass through a standard succession during which all the trees grow up together. They are generally undisturbed for the first few years of their existence and have, at that time, become a haven for a really quite interesting bird population. The spread of the hen harrier back to the Scottish mainland as well as southwards into Wales has been clearly correlated with the existence of young conifer plantations that offer a peaceful haven in so many of our hill districts. Grasshopper warblers too find them ideal, though both species abandon them long before they begin to resemble proper woodland. Species present in the early years of coniferous plantations are: meadow pipit, skylark, willow warbler, whinchat, tree pipit, linnet, wren, robin and chaffinch in that order.

By the time that the trees have grown to six feet or more the population shows marked changes with skylarks disappearing completely and a sharp and quite sudden decline in meadow pipit and whinchat. But these species can barely be considered typical of woodland in any case. At this stage in their development the dominant species are: willow warbler, chaffinch, goldcrest, robin, wren, wood-pigeon, coal tit, meadow pipit, blackbird, whitethroat, song thrush, redpoll, carrion crow, dunnock and tree pipit.

As the trees mature the forest community changes once again with the chaffinch taking over dominance along with the goldcrest, while the willow warbler is virtually eliminated. At this stage the birds are: chaffinch, goldcrest, wren, coal tit and robin together with much smaller numbers of chiffchaff, willow warbler, dunnock, blackbird and song thrush.

Thus in its three stages the dominant birds change from skylark and meadow pipit, to willow warbler and chaffinch, and to chaffinch and goldcrest. And throughout this process the dominant species do indeed dominate. It is doubtless this presence of only a few species in numbers that has led so many bird-watchers to regard plantations as 'birdless'.

Scrub

Scrub is generally regarded as an intermediate stage between heath or marsh, and mature woodland. It thus shares many species with both woods and plantations though, in its early stages, it is much nearer heath or marsh in terms of the birds that it holds.

Typically scrub consists of a broken landscape with small trees and bushes reaching less than twenty-five feet. Some of these may be woods that are in the process of growing as, for instance, plantations in areas that have been felled or coppiced. But true scrub consists of species that will never grow tall enough to create a woodland. Elder and gorse come immediately to mind, along with hawthorn, blackthorn, hazel, osier, willow and juniper. Brambles, too, frequently form a significant part of scrub.

Although the species found in scrub bear a marked similarity to those of young and intermediate plantations there are significant differences. Typical birds of dry scrub include whinchat, yellowhammer, linnet, wren, meadow pipit and greenfinch, although some highly localized species such as Dartford warbler are also found only in such habitats. Damp scrub has a slightly different bird population including sedge and marsh warblers (another highly localized species) as well as the more widespread wren and cuckoo.

The decline of the rabbit, following the introduction of myxamatosis, has led to a significant increase in the area and density of scrub and a resulting increase in the numbers of some species. However, as if to compensate, other areas of scrub are being continually cleared for agriculture.

Field Vegetation

Huge areas of Britain consist of fields of one sort or another; most common is grassland. Used either for grazing or for hay or silage, grassland is in more or less continual use throughout the year. Even when domestic animals are not present (as in many areas through the winter months) some form of maintenance, be it harvesting, raking, fertilizing or spraying, is taking place. Grassy fields are frequented by a number of ground-feeding birds such as lapwings, blackbirds and song thrushes as well as the winter visitors such as redwings and fieldfares. However, the absence of weeds in well-kept fields precludes their use by large numbers of seed-eating species and general disturbance makes them unsuitable as nest sites by most birds.

A neglected field that has a growth of long grass and a plentiful supply of grass seeds is, however, a quite different matter. Such grasslands then more resemble moorland and will provide feeding for finches such as linnets as well as a breeding niche for lapwings and skylarks. A neglected field will soon support a strong growth of nettles and thistles and is then an attraction to birds as diverse as whitethroats and goldfinches.

Much neglected grassland is quickly colonized by bracken which, though of negligible value as a food plant, is of considerable importance to many ground-nesting birds such as pheasant, partridge and nightjar. This often represents the first stage in the succession from heath or moorland to birch woodland and it is interesting that the declining nightjar is, in fact, a bird of a transitional habitat.

Upland grasslands, often grazed by sheep, are never rich but do hold several species in good numbers. Meadow pipits and skylarks spring immediately to mind, but there are merlins, wheatears, cuckoos and other species as well.

Finally there are some grasslands, situated at the very tops of Britain's highest mountains, that are virtually Alpine in character. Fescue grass, together with various lichens and mosses, is usually dominant and birds include the elusive dotterel and snow bunting.

Farms

The farm itself usually consists of groups of buildings surrounded by yards and possibly grounds that form a miniature suburb in the middle of open country. As such it has more in common with suburban gardens than the countryside, though grain spillage and slurry disposal (on dairy farms) attracts species as various as pied wagtails and collared doves. Hay and straw ricks often hold starlings and little owls, but it is the fields of crops (other than grasslands) that are the main elements in attracting birds to farms. Winter-sown cereals form an important habitat for the wild geese that flock into Britain in winter. Some of these, notably pink-feet, may then descend on potato fields to feed on the waste left in the late autumn. Spilt and wasted grain form an important part of the diet of many seed-eating birds, notably house sparrows, in late summer and combine harvesters and the practice of sub-contracting the harvest to teams, more concerned with speed than yield, only increases this wastage. A crop of rape may be alive with finches in autumn, and orchards are a happy hunting ground for thrushes galore throughout the winter months. Those same orchards may be a life-saver for tits and bullfinches at blossom time, particularly if other foods such as the crop of ash seeds have failed. Crops as varied as raspberries and broccoli are used by birds.

It is, however, the British practice of enclosing fields by hedgerows (as well as walls) that maintains our countryside bird population and variety. Although thousands of miles of such hedges are removed every year sufficient remain to form one of the most significant areas for nature in Britain. A huge variety of birds find both nesting and feeding sites in hedgerows, while birds that feed among the fields themselves invariably find cover and roosting sites in adjacent hedgerows. Species include: blackbird, song thrush, mistle thrush, whitethroat, yellow-hammer, wren, tawny owl, woodpigeon, robin, greenfinch, goldfinch, linnet and many others.

Inland Cliffs

Cliffs exist in many parts of Britain and are doubtless increasing in number. Man's search for raw materials has led him to quarry for items as varied as granite and sand and the resulting cliffs are often immediately occupied by birds. In Scotland natural cliffs are the haunt of raven, jackdaw, peregrine and golden eagle. In lowland Britain cliffs are (or were) generally rather scarce. Now sand pits are the site of some huge colonies of sand martins and there can be little doubt that the species has increased as a direct result of man's activities. In North Wales the old slate quarries are one of the very few strongholds of the elusive chough.

Sea Coasts

The nature of the British coastline, and we are fortunate in having an enormously long coast for the overall size of our islands, is as variable as the vegetation that clothes our countryside. Over the centuries the sea and tides have created scenery (and habitats) as varied as estuarine ooze and some of the world's most magnificent cliffs. All, without exception, hold birds, but these in turn are as varied as the coastline itself. The process continues so that while one coastline is being eroded another is being created. Even within the space of a few miles cliffs may be falling into the sea only to reappear 'down-tide' as an ever-increasing shingle bank.

Cliffs

Sea-cliffs are created by wave action cutting away at the base of a hill. Their nature depends entirely on the underlying geology which, in turn, determines the birds that will best be able to exploit the various opportunities for nesting. By and large cliffs are important as nest sites rather than feeding zones, though the peregrine and skuas find their food among the precipices in their different ways.

Tall, hard-based cliffs are the haunt of seabirds, particularly where their underlying structure creates ledges and crannies suitable for nest sites. At suitable spots, invariably where the offshore waters are rich in fish, thousands of birds such as guillemots, razorbills, kittiwakes and fulmars may crowd together. Among them may be black guillemots, puffins and in some areas gannets. Where such cliffs have crumbled to form a huge steep scree shags may be found occupying every nook and cranny.

Similar cliffs elsewhere may lack the wealth of an adjacent mineral-rich sea and simply support the gulls that can glean a living along the shoreline or by scavenging at some nearby seaport.

Cliffs of sand or clay may never rise to the heights required by the more typical seabirds, though fulmars have expanded in range and number to such an extent that they now occupy the strangest of nest sites at many coastal locations. There can be little doubt that sea sand cliffs must have, at one time, been the dominant habitat for sand martins, and large colonies can still be found in many parts of the country.

Some cliffs of the harder rocks frequently form offshore stacks or islets. These are particularly attractive to the auks and other typical seabirds, but are also favoured by gannets for which security seems so important.

Beaches

Almost without exception British beaches suffer from a summertime invasion of people that puts the birds that breed on them particularly at risk. There is no better example of this than the decline of the little tern, which formerly nested all around our shores wherever sand or shingle beaches could be found. This species is increasingly restricted to shingle bars where access is either restricted or where the very nature of the ground makes access difficult. As a result the little tern is now one of our rarest breeding seabirds. The ringed plover and oystercatcher both suffer from the same problem but, being more catholic in habitat, they have not significantly declined in numbers as a result.

Beaches, either of shingle or sand, are feeding grounds for a number of different species, but they are of little significance when compared with the huge intertidal banks of sand and mud that occur along many of our low-lying shores. These banks are, in contrast, among the richest of all British habitats and are best considered as extensions of the estuaries which invariably back them.

Estuaries

Twice each day the tides of Britain cover and uncover the banks of mud and sand that line the mouths of most British rivers. In some estuaries the intertidal area is huge and the ooze itself is unbelievably rich in animate life. For birds adapted to exploit this richness such estuaries are truly bountiful. Several British estuaries boast totals of over a hundred thousand waders placing them high in the rankings of European wetlands. The birds they attract vary considerably for, while almost all such sites boast a strong population of dunlin, some will have huge flocks of knot, other oystercatchers, others godwits and so on. Species involved in considerable numbers include: dunlin, knot, oystercatcher, ringed plover, bar-tailed godwit, grey plover, redshank and turnstone. At various seasons estuaries are used by greenshank, spotted redshank, ruff, black-tailed godwit, and other species that neither breed, nor winter with us.

An important element in all estuaries is the level of natural reclamation and colonization by salt tolerant plants. The areas colonized soon rise, by deposition of silt and the trapping potential of the plants, into 'saltings'. These are important as high tide roosts for waders and provide a feeding ground for large numbers of wildfowl. Brent geese and wigeon may be particularly abundant in winter at estuaries where eel grass is present in quantity. Even the open mud offers opportunities to several widlfowl, notably shelduck.

Rocky Shores

Rock outcrops occur at many points along our shores. Though they are

Top **Temminck's stint** incubating. After erratic attempts this diminutive wader now breeds regularly in small numbers in northern Scotland and may be looked for in several areas.
Bottom Open uplands and coastal marshes are the haunt of the **short-eared owl**. Though not the most numerous of species its diurnal habits make it one of the most frequently seen.

Top One of the great rarities – **Ross's gull** – that sends bird-watchers travelling huge distances for a possible sighting. This individual wandered southwards from the Arctic ice cap to Stanpit Marsh in Hampshire in 1974.
Bottom **Male bearded tit** bringing food to its young. Following a succession of good breeding seasons these attractive little birds have spread westwards from their East Anglian strongholds and may be looked for in any large reed bed in England and Wales

rich in life, as any child who has explored a rock pool will confirm, the number and variety of birds is limited. Some species are truly rocky shore specialists – purple sandpiper, turnstone and oystercatcher spring immediately to mind – and others such as redshank and dunlin find them sufficiently attractive to use in small numbers. Only the purple sandpiper is actually confined to rocky shores, but it will occupy even quite small outcrops surrounded by otherwise unsuitable habitat.

Among the duck the eider is something of a rock specialist. It feeds mainly on mussels that it obtains by diving and will also nest on rocky islets as well as among dunes. Other sea duck also feed on mussels, but they may do so offshore and are less dependent on the nature of the coastline itself.

Freshwater

The various areas of freshwater can be divided into a number of quite distinct habitats, each of which holds a characteristic bird population. Many of these habitats are quite distinctive such as pond, lake, reservoir, flood, stream, canal and river. But others such as loch, pool, mere, brook and beck are more difficult to define, save that they are often local names.

Streams

From their highest origins where they are little more than a trickle, streams develop and run fast over mainly stony bottoms. They may be called brooks or becks, but their nature is the same. In hilly districts streams may continue for miles and grow to considerable proportions. The dipper is perhaps their most typical bird, though grey wagtail and common sandpiper are also frequently present. The occasional kingfisher may be resident, but this is a more catholic species that will occupy a wide variety of aquatic habitats.

Rivers

Rivers are wider and more slow-moving than streams. The bottom has considerable amounts of mud giving rise to a strong growth of weeds, and the river will frequently meander over a flood plain. In many ways rivers are similar to ponds and the growth of emergent vegetation along their banks will shelter moorhens and coots, a few duck and, where not polluted, kingfishers. Pied wagtails, reed buntings and sedge warblers all find the banks of rivers to their liking and many other species, not confined to water, seem to find river banks attractive.

Canals

Canals are very similar to rivers, save only that their flow is remarkably slow. Most British canals were built in the eighteenth century and passed into decline within a hundred years. Many are now overgrown and silted up and provide a long, narrow aquatic environment that is virtually free from disturbance. Moorhens and coots breed in numbers together with mallards, dabchicks, pied wagtails, sedge warblers and so on.

Ponds

The village pond is an oasis, but one that is of limited use to birds. Like canals and rivers, ponds often have a strong growth of emergent vegetation, but little boys, fishermen and dogs are a source of continual disturbance and only a few pairs of moorhens and coots manage to breed. Their shallow edges are, however, a source of mud for swallows and house martins, the latter particularly finding their ideal niche in the English village.

Lakes

Most of Britain's large natural freshwaters are situated in hilly or mountain districts and are invariably deep and rather barren of life. However, a few natural lowland lakes can be found as, for instance, at Loch Leven, and these may be remarkably rich and form a haven for breeding ducks, terns, gulls and many other species. They also attract a wealth of wintering and passage birds including some quite staggering concentrations of geese and other wildfowl.

Reservoirs

Lowland Britain has gained enormously from the construction, mainly during the present century, of huge reservoirs to provide fresh water for the growing urban environment. Waters such as Grafham, Rutland and so on provide huge aquatic environments in areas that were otherwise devoid of such habitats. Their main attraction is to winter wildfowl, particularly to duck, and numbers may build up to total several thousand at peak periods. They are also handy resting and feeding sites for birds of passage, and waders and terns are invariably present at the better sites throughout migration periods. The species present tends to vary from water to water, doubtless dependent on the depth, the nature of the edge, the availability of food in the surrounding district, and other factors. But the construction of a large lowland reservoir has brought top-class bird-watching to many areas that were otherwise comparatively barren.

Gravel Pits

The use of concrete as a major construction material has led to a massive exploitation of gravel beds along lowland rivers throughout the country. Invariably such pits are flooded as soon as the waterline is breached and they quickly turn into gravel-fringed lagoons. Even while they are being worked little ringed plovers will move in and breed and the colonization of Britain by that attractive newcomer has been closely correlated with the creation of new gravel workings. At the end of their working life gravel pits were formerly fenced and forgotten, but in these more enlightened days proper schemes for reconstitution are required before planning permission to excavate a new site is given. Such is the demand for water for leisure that fishing, water skiing, sailing, power boating and other aquatic pursuits all compete for disused pits. These activities are organized through clubs that are prepared to pay highly for their sport. Bird-watchers are indeed fortunate that reconstitution plans invariably involve some form of provision for conservation if they are to be accepted. Thus a nature reserve is invariably included in such plans.

Gravel pits are a major habitat for the great crested grebe, for wintering duck, and for species as diverse as sedge warblers and coots. A good reserve that includes a decent area of margin and hinterland will produce a wealth of breeding species.

Floods

For generations farmers have attempted, usually with considerable success, to prevent the swollen rivers of winter from spilling over their banks and flooding the adjacent grassland. Yet many river valleys still have splashy areas in winter and some are still liable to quite extensive flooding. These floods are remarkably attractive to birds and form a quite distinctive habitat throughout the year. In winter surface-feeding duck may descend by their thousand along with waders and, in some places, geese and wild swans. The Ouse Washes are notable in this respect, but they are far from unique.

In summer these same meadows dry out and are then home to many species including black-tailed godwit, ruff and yellow wagtail.

Marsh

Marshes vary enormously from upland and rather barren bogs, to coastal lagoons that provide one of the richest environments for birds. There are acid marshes, reed marshes, overgrown tangles of willow and sallow, salt marshes and freshwater marshes. Each has its typical bird community, though some have already been dealt with elsewhere in this chapter. Marshes are characterized by shallow water throughout the year and their vegetation depends on the degree of salinity (if any), the actual depth of water, and their age. Like all habitats, save for the forest climax, marshes are forever changing and must be managed if they are to survive in a particular state.

Taking the example of a typical east coast marsh the whole range of marsh-type vegetation can be examined. Behind the beach a series of semi-saline lagoons is maintained by salt water leaching in from the sea. This prevents the growth of all but a few salt-tolerant plants and maintains the lagoons as open feeding grounds for waders, shelduck, wigeon, teal and other duck. Gradually the level of salinity declines as one moves inland and fresh marshes offer opportunities for a stronger growth of vegetation and for birds such as migrant wood sandpipers and ruff. These marshes may easily become overgrown with reeds and form the huge beds beloved of bearded tits, bitterns, marsh harriers, reed warblers, sedge warblers and colonizing Savi's warblers. Several of these species occur nowhere else, save for the inland broads which are so similar in ecological terms. Reeds, in their turn, are invaded by willow scrub and by birch, and will gradually become choked, giving an opportunity for other trees to grow and form a fen where, of the aquatic species, only woodcock will prosper.

Such a brief note cannot do justice to such a rich habitat and one that clearly merits a book of its own. Nevertheless, a marsh, wherever found, is an immense attraction to bird-watchers. Of course, not all marshes are coastal. The Norfolk Broads are the result of old peat diggings and form one of the most important of wetland habitats in Britain. Stodmarsh and Fairburn Ings have been formed as a result of mining subsidence and bring marshland habitat to what were previously impoverished areas. The 'Scrape' at Minsmere is a result of direct human construction in converting a few pools and some rough grassland into a bird marsh. It is a process that could, given sufficient funds, be repeated in many parts of Britain.

Towns and Cities

With the notable exceptions of swift and black redstart, towns and cities are not rich in birds. Feeders, nest boxes and bird gardening may all help to make them more attractive and, as a result, the suburban garden may boast a higher density of breeding birds than any other habitat. But the level of species is generally rather low. A city park may be an oasis for migrants in a sea of concrete, but unusual birds are few and far between. It is interesting that virtually any urban open space will produce migrants, but the interest lies in the fact that the birds occur at all, not in any interest for their own sake.

Swifts find the suburbs, with their wealth of breeding sites, ideal; and black redstarts, after initially colonizing city centre bomb and construction sites, have moved into sidings and shunting yards.

The paraphernalia of urban life, the need for water and for rubbish and sewage disposal, provides some excellent opportunities for birds, though generally in somewhat unsalubrious places. Rubbish tips attract scavengers, particularly winter gulls, and sewage works offer 'marshes' to passage waders. Often these are the best spots available to the non-travelling urban bird-watcher, but a strong stomach is usually required.

HOT SPOTS

Certain spots are better for birds than others, or at least bird-watchers think they are and, by concentrating sufficient binocular power, make their belief come true. Though these 'hot spots' are seasonably variable, the very best are good throughout the year and are thronged by their supporters weekend after weekend. Others are mainly autumn places, the rush season for birds and their watchers. Others still are predominantely winter spots, with a relatively stable population of birds, that birders can pop into and out of over a considerable period of time without feeling that they have missed anything. Inevitably a choice of such places is purely personal, for though many are now reserves, the turnstile approach with attendance figures has yet to penetrate bird-watching. Nevertheless I would bet that my list of eighteen hot spots includes most people's favourites as well as those most frequented.

Apart from the actual field sport of birding, bird-watchers get a great deal of fun, and sometimes satisfaction, from what can only be called rarity speculation. This harmless pursuit involves assessing the chances of unknown and unvisited sites holding rare birds. Thus with Fair Isle, which is a known hot spot, the Out Skerries of Shetland nearby would seem an obvious place, and so it has proved. My own favourite was the north-eastern tip of Unst, also in the Shetlands, and it provided a spring woodchat shrike within two days of watching as a reward.

Others have had spectacular success in various parts of the country. Porthgawarra near Land's End was unheard of until it started producing some of the species in search of which birders had flooded past on their autumn trek to the Isles of Scilly. Now it is almost a compulsory stop-over. The Butt of Lewis in the Outer Hebrides proved good for goose migration, but what other birds would find it such an attractive landfall? Working one's way around the coasts of Britain on a map, one cannot help but speculate on the chances of a real hot spot having been hitherto overlooked.

The lesson is easily learned – what follows is a list of places where other people have regularly seen exciting birds, not a list of where such birds regularly occur. Unfortunately we shall not be able to compile that list until all unusual birds have, by law, to declare themselves on entering the country. Perhaps we have touched upon the very heart of the attraction of birds – that in an age of increasing restrictions and controls on our behaviour, birds are able to ignore all frontiers, boundaries and regulations and continue on their way with let or hindrance from no one.

Hot spots are listed alphabetically:

Aberlady Bay
This lies on the southern shore of the Firth of Forth east of Edinburgh whose birders flock to watch over its mud banks for rare waders. Generally produces at least one decent rarity a year, with many other good birds particularly in autumn.

Blackpill
This extraordinary area on the coast of Glamorgan boasts a huge gull roost among which enthusiasts have managed to find a succession of ring-billed gulls, vagrants from North America. To date no other area in Britain has been able even to offer a challenge to the Welsh predominance of records of this species. Strangely, despite the hours of highly skilled searching, very few other rare birds have been revealed.

Cley and Blakeney
North Norfolk Mecca with the highest bird-watcher concentrations year in, year out, of any spot in Britain. Regularly produces rare and unusual birds, but also has excellent populations of the more common, but valued, species. The east bank at Cley runs to the sea and watchers often gather to talk away summer afternoons overlooking Arnold's Marsh to the east. Blakeney Point is less frequented, but always has something in the autumn.

Dungeness
The site of an old-established bird reserve and of the more recent nuclear power station, 'Dunge', as it is affectionately known, is one of the most unsalubrious places in Britain to watch birds. Unfortunately it

also boasts birds as varied as rare warblers and unusual terns and gulls attracted by the hot water outlet of the power station known (also affectionately) as 'The Patch'.

Fair Isle
Isolated between Shetland and Orkney, Fair Isle discovered rare birds long before 'twitchers' were invented. With a string of first records for Britain to its credit and an even longer one of 'specialities' seldom found elsewhere in the country, it is not surprising that bird-watchers descend in their droves at peak migration times. Autumn, particularly August and September, is the busiest period and it is difficult to imagine a fortnight at that time when at least one major rarity is not spotted.

Gibraltar Point
The site of a long-established and well-organised bird observatory and field centre, this peninsula at the northern corner of The Wash regularly attracts a wide variety of birds among which the occasional rarity occurs.

Holkham and Wells
Situated at the centre of the highly favoured north coast of Norfolk and with an excellent level of cover, Holkham has produced more than its share of rarities in recent years. It now forms part of the itinerary of any bird-watcher visiting this coast and is best in late autumn when unusual leaf warblers may be present. Wells is a pleasant little port a mile or so inland and is a haunt of geese and other waterbirds.

Holme
A nice little reserve of marsh and shore at the southern mouth of The Wash, Holme is the site of a bird observatory and produces a fair variety of unusual and rare birds at all seasons. Some top rate rarities have occurred here.

Isle of May
One of the oldest established and best loved of all bird observatories. Situated in the Firth of Forth its drawing power would seem to be limited, yet year after year it turns up a selection of rarities as exciting as almost anywhere in the country.

Minsmere
Situated on the Suffolk coast and high spot of the RSPB's create-a-

habitat campaign, Minsmere is now perhaps the most visited bird spot in Britain. Top rate breeding birds tend to overshadow the considerable number of rarities turned up by a band of enthusiasts who regularly include a scan of 'The Scrape' in their East Anglian week-ends. Waders are best here, but the bushes at 'The Sluice' hold the occasional passerine rarity.

Ouse Washes
This Cambridgeshire wetland is not so much a hot spot as a predictable supplier of some of the very best bird-watching in Britain. In summer the Washes, much of which comprise RSPB and Wildfowl Trust reserves, are a haunt of several species of waders including ruff and black-tailed godwit. In winter they are frequented by wild swans and hosts of ducks. Seldom a rarity but good value birds at all seasons.

Portland
The site of an excellent bird observatory and field centre near Weymouth, and one of the best rarity sites and seabird observation points on the south coast. An extensive trapping programme produces many of the best passerines, but seabird migration includes some really first class birds such as Cory's shearwater in season.

Radipole
An exquisite little marsh on the edge of the south coast town of Weymouth and virtually *en route* for those proceeding to Portland Bird Observatory. It consists of some shallow, reed-fringed lagoons that regularly attract a variety of rare birds almost irrespective of season.

St. Ives Island
Though surrounded by some excellent year-round bird-watching sites including the equisite Hayle estuary, St. Ives in Cornwall is best in September and October when westerly gales blow seabirds onshore to the mouth of the Severn. Shearwaters and gulls may then be found sheltering in the bay, but are best seen as they battle their way back into the open Atlantic tight around the headland that is called an island. At other times it is barely worth a visit.

Isles of Scilly
Only a few years ago the Isles of Scilly were thought of as a rival to Fair Isle in the number of true vagrants that they produced. Now, it could be argued, they have taken over the mantle. Late September and October

sees hundreds of twitchers combing every nook and cranny for the rarities that continue to appear. The inter-island telephone is alive with twitchers' gossip every evening, and the local boats do a roaring trade as watchers commute from island to island with each new bird. American birds are a speciality, but anything may turn up. If you can stand the crowds the birding can be amazing.

Isle of Sheppey

Situated at the mouth of the Thames estuary, Sheppey has for long been a regular haunt of London-based bird-watchers. However, recent years have seen its reputation spreading more widely and it has become something of a classic area for winter birds. It has an RSPB reserve, some excellent marshes, and a wildfowl and wader population of international importance. Hen harriers and rough-legged buzzards are so regular in the bitter months of winter that bird-watchers are often present in their droves.

Spurn

The tip of the Spurn peninsula is the site of a well-established bird observatory and the resort of many Yorkshire-based bird-watchers. Good birds are always present, but in autumn wader and seabird watching is among the best on the east coast. Passerine migration of the more usual 'Scandinavian' type species is frequently abundant and birds rare enough to send twitchers scurrying across the country turn up from time to time.

Walberswick

Often overlooked in the mad dash to nearby Minsmere, the marshes at Walberswick are among the very best in the country. The wealth of exciting breeding birds is barely inferior to that of its more famous neighbour and only 'under-watching' prevents it producing an equal number of rarities during migration seasons. When, as on occasion, it has been intensively watched it has produced some really outstanding birds. The winter raptor population is as good here as anywhere in the country.

THE BIRDS

Red-throated Diver *Gavia stellata*

Resident: This attractive diver breeds on small lochs and lochans among the Highlands of Scotland where its rust-red throat patch makes it easily identifiable. In winter it resorts to sea-coasts, loses its distinguishing features, but can still be easily identified by the pronounced uptilt to its head and bill. At all seasons it is the most plentiful member of its family.
Habitat: Lochs, with or without islands, often quite small but always near a larger water or the sea where it can fish. In winter along coasts.
Locations: Northern and western Scotland where a population of some 700-plus pairs can be found from April to October. Most numerous north of the Caledonian Canal and quite abundant in the Shetlands; 100 pairs (40 pairs on Unst).
Winter Visitor: Quite numerous around most coasts though absent from the north of Scotland and the islands. Large flocks sometimes build up at particularly favoured feeding grounds. There is a pronounced spring passage up-Channel along the south coast.
Locations: Selsey and Dungeness in late March and April for passage; winters most coasts from Cornwall to Firth of Forth, but also in west. Occasionally inland at large reservoirs.

Black-throated Diver *Gavia arctica*

Resident: Enjoys a circumpolar breeding distribution in high latitudes and is called 'arctic loon' in North America where, however, it is replaced over large areas in the west by the Pacific loon which is sometimes considered conspecific. It inhabits the Highland districts of

Scotland but is quite scarce with a total population of less than 200 pairs. In winter, like the other divers, it resorts to coasts where, however, it is always outnumbered by the red-throated diver. Most likely to be confused with great northern diver in winter, but the latter is larger and has much heavier head and bill.

Habitat: In summer inhabits large lochs with islets where it can find sufficient food without commuting, a contrast with the smaller hill lochs occupied by the red-throated diver. In winter frequents inshore waters and bays.

Locations: Though the black-throated diver breeds along the west coast of Scotland from Arran and Kintyre it is distinctly more common north of the Caledonian Canal. Wester Ross – at Torridon and Strath Polly – and Sutherland are the strongholds of the species. Expect to walk rough country exploring large and remote lochs.

Winter Visitor: Winter visitors arrive in September and stay through to April.

Locations: Scottish coasts are most frequented, but the east coast of England has many regular haunts such as Lindisfarne, Teesmouth, Spurn, The Wash, Cley; and there are always some birds along the south coast at places like Rye Harbour, Pagham, Langstone, etc. Inland it is mainly storm driven, but tough weather may bring it to the larger London reservoirs.

Great Northern Diver *Gavia immer*

Resident: After generations of speculation and rumour the great northern diver was finally proved to have bred in Wester Ross in 1970. Elsewhere it breeds only in Iceland and across North America where its name 'common loon' indicates its status.

Habitat: Large lakes with islands and islets in varying surroundings; in winter at sea near suitable coastlines,

Locations: One spot in Wester Ross and another to the south which remain secret. However, summering great northerns can regularly be seen in Shetland particularly off Yell, Unst and Fetlar.

Winter Visitor: In Europe the species is essentially a winter visitor from Iceland and perhaps Greenland, to Scandinavian and British shores and southwards to Brittany and Portugal. It can be quite numerous and is regular in many parts of Scotland.

Locations: Shetland; the Minches between the Outer Hebrides and the mainland where it is numerous; Irish Sea coasts of Lancashire and North Wales; Cornwall; south-east England and North Norfolk. Very scarce inland.

White-billed Diver *Gavia adamsii*

Winter Visitor: This large arctic-based diver is now established as a regular winter visitor to Britain in small numbers each year. It is easily confused with the great northern diver which is also a winter visitor, but more plentiful. The uptilted look to the bill is the most reliable field mark, though some great northerns have a remarkably similar–shaped bill.

Habitat: At sea in inshore waters outside the breeding season.

Locations: This is a scarce bird with no regular haunts. It can, however, be looked for along the east coast of Scotland and northern England from January to March and further north in the Shetlands in April and May.

Little Grebe *Tachybaptus ruficollis*

Resident: One of the most widespread of all the world's birds, the little grebe, or dabchick, is widespread throughout the country and absent only from the highest hills. It is, nevertheless, easily overlooked particularly during the breeding season when it submerges at the slightest sign of danger and disappears completely by re-emerging among dense cover. Some 7,000 to 15,000 pairs breed in Britain.

Habitat: Ponds and lakes with plentiful growth of vegetation, marshes and canals, dykes and slow-moving streams and rivers. In winter occurs on reservoirs, estuaries and other large waters.

Locations: Virtually everywhere outside the hill districts of the north and west.

Great Crested Grebe *Podiceps cristatus*

Resident: Down to 32 pairs by 1860, the great crested grebe has made a spectacular recovery and now numbers about 5,000 pairs spread over the lowland districts of England, Wales and Scotland. It is absent from the Highlands, the border country and the Pennines, from west Wales and the south-west; elsewhere it is widespread and comparatively obvious. The protection afforded by a series of Acts at the end of last century made it comparatively oblivious of human company and it now nests on town and city park ponds, and even in gravel pits that are still being worked.

Habitat: Ponds, lakes and more recently slow moving streams with, or without, islets and some emergent vegetation. It can form colonies under ideal conditions. Winters on large waters, especially reservoirs, as well as long sheltered coasts.

Locations: Breeding birds are widespread and occupy even quite small waters. Most densely occupied counties are Norfolk, Essex, Hertfordshire, Buckinghamshire, Shropshire, Staffordshire, Cheshire, Warwickshire and Nottinghamshire. Most of these have benefitted from the growth of the gravel extraction industry.

Winter Visitor: Concentrates on large, mainly man-made, waters in winter with good flocks at the Midland and London reservoirs, e.g., Rutland, Grafham, Eyebrook, Staines, Datchet, Barn Elms, Walthamstow, William Girling; as well as at Chew, Weir Wood and others.

Red-necked Grebe *Podiceps grisegena*

Winter Visitor: Though the occasional red-necked grebe does spend the summer in Britain, it is as a winter visitor in small numbers that the species is best known.

Habitat: In winter found mainly on coastal waters, but also inland on large reservoirs.

Locations: From the Firth of Forth southwards along the east and south coasts this species is a scarce winter visitor. Lindisfarne and north Norfolk usually have their fair quota and Pagham is a favoured haunt. Inland the larger London reservoirs often produce a singleton, though nowhere could these birds be said to be regular.

Slavonian Grebe *Podiceps auritus*

Resident: This attractive grebe has a circumpolar breeding distribution and is known as the 'horned grebe' (a better name?) in North America. In Britain it is confined to the Scottish Highlands where the main population is remarkably concentrated. Egg collectors, as with so many other rare species, preclude the exact whereabouts being published.

Habitat: Large shallow freshwater lochs of an acidic nature with some emergent vegetation, surrounded by heather moorland. In winter found mostly in estuaries and along shorelines, though also inland on large reservoirs.

Locations: It is no secret that the main colony of Slavonian grebes in Britain is centred on a group of lochs in Inverness south of the Caledonian Canal, and has about 40 pairs. However, there are also good numbers to the north.

Winter Visitor: A scattering of Slavonian grebes can be found from September to March in many coastal areas, but beware confusion with similar black-necked grebe.

Locations: Regular spots include the north Norfolk coast and Lindisfarne, but there are also singles at many smaller estuaries. Inland it is a visitor to some large reservoirs including Staines.

Black-necked Grebe *Podiceps nigricollis*

Resident: Only a handful of pairs of this delightful little grebe breed in Britain, with only a few more in Ireland. At one time no less than 250 pairs bred at a single water in that country, but drainage destroyed Lough Funshinagh for ever. Colonies up to a dozen strong come and go, but there are no more than four regular British and Irish spots. Elsewhere it frequently nests among large marsh-based colonies of black-headed gulls.

Habitat: Rich lowland lakes and marshes with a good growth of emergent vegetation.

Locations: There is a colony in the lowlands of Scotland.

Winter Visitor: Elsewhere the black-necked grebe is a winter visitor and passage migrant to our coasts and estuaries and, in smaller numbers, to our larger inland waters. Staines Reservoir has a small gathering in late summer from August to October that is as regular as any in the country. It is decidedly rare north of The Wash and in the west.

Fulmar *Fulmarus glacialis*

Resident: Once confined to a few isolated sub-arctic islands, the fulmar has spread over a large area of the North Atlantic during the last hundred years and can now be found along virtually every coast of Britain.

Habitat: Rocky cliffs along coasts, though in the north of Scotland it also occupies old ruined buildings and cliffs some distance from the sea. At other times largely pelagic.

Locations: Huge numbers breed around the cliff-lined coasts of Britain and it is particularly numerous in the far north in Shetland and Orkney where virtually any ledge or crevice will suffice as a nest. Further south colonies tend to be more scattered and Lancashire, Lincolnshire, Suffolk and Essex are devoid of breeding birds. In the south-east, Hampshire, Sussex and Kent have very few colonies. However, even such low-lying coasts regularly have prospecting birds every spring and summer and the fulmar is present throughout the year not far offshore. Truly huge colonies in excess of 10,000 pairs at St. Kilda, Fair Isle, Foula, Fetlar and Hermaness.

Cory's Shearwater *Calonectris diomedea*

Passage Migrant: A large shearwater that breeds at colonies throughout the Mediterranean and among many of the island groups in the eastern Atlantic. At the end of the breeding season it spreads out across the North Atlantic reaching the rich fishing grounds of eastern North America, and southwards to the Cape of Good Hope. Its northern limit just reaches the southern tip of Ireland and birds are sometimes blown up-Channel to south-western England.

Habitat: Open seas; breeds on rocky often uninhabited islands.

Locations: Isles of Scilly, St. Ives, The Lizard, Start Point, Portland Bill; pelagic trips into the mouth of the Channel between late June and early October would doubtless reveal more birds.

Great Shearwater *Puffinus gravis*

Passage Migrant: Large, well-marked shearwater that nests only on the islands of the Tristan da Cunha group and (ocassionally or rarely) on the Falkland Islands. After breeding, the birds, which number about $2\frac{1}{2}$

million pairs, make a huge loop migration into the North Atlantic where they arrive on the Grand Banks in May. Later they cross the Atlantic eastwards and may be very common in the Bay of Biscay northwards to Scotland from July to September.

Habitat: Open seas; uninhabited islands.

Locations: Outer Hebrides, Cornwall, Isles of Scilly, Portland.

Sooty Shearwater *Puffinus griseus*

Passage Migrant: Breeds only in the southern parts of the Southern Hemisphere in the regions of New Zealand and Patagonia. Outside the breeding season spreads over the southern oceans and northwards into the North Pacific and North Atlantic. These huge journeys regularly bring birds to all British coasts.

Habitat: Open seas; breeds on islands, often at some altitude.

Locations: Most coasts except the south-east. Occasional in spring, but regular in August and September; most often seen in the north-west and south-west, but is regular off North Sea coasts at places like Teesmouth and Spurn. Regular around fishing boats.

Manx Shearwater *Puffinus puffinus*

Summer Visitor: Though it breeds at several extremely large colonies this predominantly pelagic species is virtually unknown on many long stretches of coastline. In contrast it is often locally abundant in the region of its colonies and some areas produce staggering numbers: between 175,000 and 300,000 pairs.

Habitat: Uninhabited islands, rocky promontories, mountain tops, otherwise offshore and pelagic. Spends most of its year out of sight of land.

Locations: Breeding colonies at several places along western coasts; largest colonies are at Skockholm and Skomer, and at Rhum and Eigg. Other well-established but smaller colonies at Isles of Scilly, Lundy, Bardsey, Calf of Man, Hoy in Orkney, Foula and Fetlar in Shetland. Colonies doubtless exist in both Inner and Outer Hebrides and probably in Anglesey and Gwynedd, and the Farnes.

Passage Migrant: Birds passing to and from their breeding grounds often participate in spectacular movements. Huge numbers can sometimes be seen off the Isles of Scilly and the Minches are frequently alive with birds. The western Mediterranean form *P.p. mauretanicus* is a regular late summer visitor in small numbers to British waters particularly in the south-west. July to October are best months.
Locations: St. Agnes, Isles of Scilly; the Minches from Oban to Outer Hebrides – seen best from the steamer; for *P.p. mauretanicus* Portland Bill and other Channel promontories.

Storm Petrel *Hydrobates pelagicus*

Summer Visitor: A small and elusive oceanic bird that comes to land only after dark to visit its breeding colonies all of which are situated on small, generally uninhabited islands. If missed at breeding colonies it may be seen at sea from a boat, or occasionally storm-driven along coasts and even inland, usually in November. Sometimes large numbers may be 'wrecked' by strong storms.
Habitat: Isolated islands where it nests in cliffs, among rocks, or in burrows. At other seasons keeps well away from land.
Locations: More or less confined to the west coast where almost all breeding colonies are located and from which most 'wrecks' derive. A string of colonies, some of which are quite substantial, stretches from Shetland through Orkney to the Inner and Outer Hebrides, with good colonies at Fetlar, Foula, Fair Isle and Anskerry in Orkney. It breeds on the outliers of Sula Sgeir, Sule Skerry and North Rona; and on the Flannans and St. Kilda. Large and much more accessible colonies exist on Skokholm and Skomer and there are some among the Isles of Scilly. There may be an isolated east coast colony on the Bass Rock.

Leach's Petrel *Oceanodroma leucorhoa*

Summer Visitor: A small oceanic bird that is both rarer and even more localized than the storm petrel. It comes to land only after dark and all of its colonies are situated on very remote, mostly uninhabited islands.
Habitat: Uninhabited, virtually oceanic islands, where it nests in burrows or crevices among rocks.
Locations: Recent breeding colonies found only on Foula, Sula Sgeir, North Rona, the Flannan Islands and St. Kilda. Has bred in the past or

may do at Sule Skerry, Foula, the Monarch Isles and Berneray as well as on Rhum in the Inner Hebrides. As viewing this species on its breeding grounds inevitably requires an overnight stay, St. Kilda would appear to offer the best chance.

Passage Migrant: Leach's petrels pass along the west coasts of Britain in good numbers between September and November each year. They usually keep well out of sight of land, but autumn storms sometimes drive large numbers onshore and even 'wreck' them inland.

Locations: The occurrences of 'wrecked' birds are too unpredictable to specify locations, but the mouth of the Cheshire Dee regularly gathers up storm-driven birds in the Irish Sea area and St. Ives Island in Cornwall is another haven from north-westerly storms.

Gannet *Sula bassana*

Resident: A large and obvious seabird whose breeding headquarters in the eastern Atlantic are largely centred on the British Isles. Though it can be seen from most coasts at most times of the year, its concentration into comparatively few large breeding colonies makes for spectacular bird-watching.

Habitat: Cliffs of small offshore islands with smaller colonies on mainland cliffs.

Locations: The most accessible gannetry must be that on the mainland cliffs at Bempton in Yorkshire, but less than 100 pairs breed. Others with numbers of pairs are: St. Kilda 52,000; Flannan Islands 16; Sula Sgeir 900; Sule Stack 4,000; Hermaness 6,000; Noss 4,300; Bass Rock 9,000; Scar Rocks 450; Alisa Craig 13,000; Grassholm 16,000.

Passage Migrant: Gannets are offshore birds that wander over the North Atlantic Ocean, but they are most numerous not far from land. Huge numbers pass along the coasts of Britain to their feeding and wintering grounds in Biscay and off the coasts of Spain and Portugal.

Locations: In spring and autumn they may be very numerous off major headlands that project into their path from Cape Wrath in the extreme north-west to Portland Bill in the south.

Cormorant *Phalacrocorax carbo*

Resident: The cormorant is a common sight along all British coasts and on our estuaries and river mouths. It is, however, much more common in the north and west and is more or less absent as a regular breeder from Flamborough Head to the Isle of Wight. Though it is found at many inland waters it breeds inland only in the Scottish border country and Highlands in any numbers.

Habitat: Cliff-bound shores and islets, isolated stacks. In winter frequents all coastal seas and is particularly fond of large estuaries with plenty of fish. Inland on large lakes and reservoirs.

Locations: There are three times as many cormorants in Scotland than England, where there are less than in Wales. Largest numbers are found on the north shore of the Solway, in the Outer Hebrides, in Orkney and Shetland and especially in Caithness, where nearly 1,000 pairs breed. Largest English concentrations are in Northumberland, south Devon and the Isle of Wight.

Passage Migrant and Winter Visitor: Continental birds regularly pass through south-east England and winter alongside British birds which disperse from their breeding colonies. Local movements often take small parties flying along the shoreline.

Shag *Phalacrocorax aristotelis*

Resident: Shags have a similar life style to cormorants and may be confused with those larger birds. They are, however, even more strictly marine, only found inland when storm-driven, and confined to rocky coasts in the north and west. Between the Farne Islands and the Isle of Wight there is only one regular shaggery. Similarly it is absent from the Solway south to Great Ormes Head. Nevertheless shags do wander along all coasts and, taking sand-eels and being less dependent on flat fish than cormorants, are less confined to estuaries.

Habitat: Rocky shores, islands, broken seashore screes. In winter found off all shores.

Locations: There are ten times as many shags in Scotland as in England and over half of those are found in Orkney and Shetland. Indeed a third of the total shag population of Britain is found in Shetland. The numbers at Foula, Unst and Fetlar have to be seen to be believed, and a boat trip beneath the northern cliffs of the latter reveals a huge cascading scree of large broken boulders that is literally a shag city. Additionally there are good colonies in both Inner and Outer Hebrides and on the Bass Rock, and over a third of the English total breeds in the Isles of Scilly.

Bittern *Botaurus stellaris*

Resident: By 1870 the bittern was extinct as a British breeding bird, but by 1900 it was back in Norfolk and was proved to breed in 1911. It then slowly increased and spread, and numbers apparently reached a peak in the mid-1950s. Since then it has declined and now numbers about 30 pairs in England and Wales. Various suggestions have been offered to explain the decline including disturbance by coypus, pesticides, drainage, reed cutting – none are totally convincing.

Habitat: Large, unbroken reed-beds are a crucial requirement and most of the country's bitterns are fortunately found within the protective boundaries of nature reserves. Its presence is best noted by the male's loud booming call, for it seldom ventures out into the open and still less often takes to the air.

Locations: Bitterns breed regularly in Norfolk and Suffolk where some 65% of British birds are found. There are also well-established populations in Kent, Somerset, Yorkshire and Lancashire. Observable locations include Cley (Norfolk NT), Hickling (Norfolk NT), Leighton Moss (RSPB), Minsmere (RSPB), Stodmarsh (NNR), Walberswick (NNR).

Winter Visitor: Being particularly prone to freezing conditions, Continental bitterns wander to this country in small numbers every winter. Many must join our resident birds, but they are found in several other areas, even in small reed beds quite unsuited to breeding.

Little Bittern *Ixobrychus minutus*

Vagrant: A summer visitor to most of continental Europe that frequently overshoots to end up in Britain. Although rumour is rife there is no fully documented case of the species breeding with us, though summering birds are quite regular. However, it is an easily overlooked bird that will eventually be proved to breed.

Habitat: Large and small reed beds often near open water.

Locations: Reed beds near the south coast, particularly the south-east, in Kent and Sussex, are by far the most likely spots to produce both breeding birds and overshooting individuals from mid-April through to early June. Individuals wandering in autumn are more widespread with bird centres like north Norfolk picking up their share of vagrants.

Night Heron *Nycticorax nycticorax*

Vagrant: A virtually cosmopolitan heron that, as its name implies, is most active at night and spends its days quietly roosting in trees or shrubs where it is easily overlooked. Nevertheless it is regularly found in Britain, mostly in April as a result of overshooting during spring migration. It has, however, been recorded in every month of the year. Better called the 'black-crowned night-heron'.
Habitat: Marshes with trees, shallow fresh waters, river banks.
Locations: There has been a free-flying colony at Edinburgh Zoo since 1950 that places a doubt on any bird seen in that region. In spring the Isles of Scilly and Kent are favoured, but a bird may appear anywhere along the south coast.

Little Egret *Egretta garzetta*

Vagrant: A resident in southern Europe, but a summer visitor further north that regularly overshoots in spring to reach Britain. Recent years have seen a considerable increase in numbers and in some years the influx has reached considerable proportions. More effective protection in southern Europe may partly explain this phenomenon.
Habitat: Marshes, lakes, salt pans, river margins and other areas of shallow water.
Locations: Spring migration from the second half of April till at least mid-June produces most of the birds which are widespread along the south coast and East Anglia. Most marshy birding spots from the Isles of Scilly to The Wash have produced a little egret in their time.

Grey Heron *Ardea cinerea*

Resident: The largest resident heron and the only species likely to be seen regularly in most parts of the country. It is a widespread bird in the

Old World breeding across the Palearctic from Ireland to Japan, in Africa, and throughout much of Asia as far south as Java. The British and Irish population has been counted annually since 1928 and the fluctuations revealed have added considerably to our knowledge of bird populations in general. However, the Atlas Project of the BTO revealed some 770 new heronries indicating a population of 6,500 to 11,500 pairs for Britain and Ireland combined.

Habitat: Usually nests in trees, but in Scotland uses other sites to a greater extent. Frequents all waters that contain fish; estuaries, lakes, rivers, streams, marshes, ditches.

Locations: Breeds in every British county, though distinctly scarce in the far north and virtually absent from Shetland. Highest numbers are found among the marshes of Norfolk and Suffolk though it is a poor estuary that lacks a heron.

Winter Visitor: Scandinavian and Dutch grey herons regularly winter in Britain in some numbers.

Locations: Mostly east coast, but indistinguishable from resident population.

Purple Heron *Ardea purpurea*

Vagrant: The status of this southern and eastern heron is liable to change because of the increasing regularity with which it is occurring in Britain and the fact that it may soon be proved to breed. It is a summer visitor that exhibits the overshooting phenomenon shown by so many European herons, but which, being more or less geographically confined to the south-east of the country, may be properly considered true migration.

Habitat: Frequents large, undisturbed reed beds where it nests semi-colonially among the reeds; it does not join mixed tree heronries.

Locations: Recorded mostly between late April and June with a much less pronounced peak in August and September. Minsmere and Stodmarsh are the best spots, but the Isles of Scilly and Cley are also good.

Spoonbill *Platalea leucorodia*

Passage Migrant: Once a breeding bird, the spoonbill is now only a scarce migrant to Britain and is decidedly uncommon elsewhere in western Europe. It still nests at several places in Holland and it is doubtless from these colonies that the British migrants derive. May through to June are the best months, with some birds occasionally lingering sufficiently long to raise hopes of breeding.

Habitat: Marshes with shrubs or trees, lagoons, river margins, lakes, reed beds.

Locations: Minsmere and Cley have more spoonbills than any other British locations, and the former sometimes boasts a small flock in late May.

Mute Swan *Cygnus olor*

Resident: Arguably the world's heaviest flying bird, the mute swan is both numerous and widespread and has probably bred in every county in the country. Protected by both royal decree and exaggerated tales of its physical abilities, the swan has prospered, though its aggressiveness toward other wildfowl does not make it welcome on all waters.

Habitat: Rivers, lakes, ponds, reservoirs, marshes; seldom on the sea.

Locations: Mute swans sometimes form colonies as at the famous swannery at Abbotsbury where 500 pairs breed and concentrations of up to 1,000 are regular. Other large populations exist on Loch Bee in South Uist and on the Stour in Essex. Good winter concentrations can be seen at Christchurch, Langstone and Chichester, the London reservoirs, the Broads, Hornsea, Grafham, Eyebrook, Lindisfarne, Loch Leven and Loch of Strathbeg.

Bewick's Swan *Cygnus columbianus*

Winter Visitor: One of two wild swans that regularly visit Britain, Bewick's is smaller and has a smaller area of yellow on the bill than the whooper. It breeds in Novaya Zemlya and adjacent coasts of Siberia and the entire population west of the Taimyr comes to Europe in winter. It was formerly numerous and widespread in Scotland, but from the 1930's onwards has deserted the north in favour of wintering grounds in southern England.

Habitat: Tundra marshes; flooded grasslands, lakes and reservoirs, and also wetlands where artifical feeding routines attract the birds.

Locations: About 2,000 Bewick's winter in Britain, 1,000 of which frequent the Ouse Washes where the Wildfowl Trust have a well fed display area. October to mid-March is the season, but peak numbers usually occur in the New Year. Another large concentration is at Slimbridge where up to 500 flock in for the cereals provided in the Wildfowl Trust's pens. There are, however, a few places where these swans still occur in 'natural' surroundings including the Derwent Floods 250, Breydon Water, Eyebrook, Nene Washes and Loch of Strathbeg.

Whooper Swan *Cygnus cygnus*

Winter Visitor: A large 'wild' swan that breeds in the north in Iceland, Scandinavia and Siberia, and winters right across temperate Europe. Three-quarters of the Icelandic population moves to Britain and forms the vast majority of our wintering birds. They are widely scattered in suitable habitats in Scotland and a few places in northern England. Small numbers of Scandinavian birds have wintered in East Anglia over the last decade. The occasional pair stays on to breed in northern Scotland.
Habitat: Tundra marshes and lakes; winters on large lakes, reservoirs and estuaries.
Locations: Largest concentrations of over 200 birds occur soon after arrival in late October. At this time important localities are Loch of Strathbeg, about 500; Loch Bee; Loch Leven; Flanders Moss and Lindisfarne. Later birds can be found at many lowland lochs in central and eastern Scotland as well as on the Solway at Kirkconnell, about 100. Reliable spots include Cameron Reservoir, Ythan, Beauly Firth, Cromarty Firth, Loch Eye, Loch Fleet, Aberlady Bay, Castle Semple Loch, Carsebreck Curling Ponds, Loch of Lintrathen, Loch Spiggie.

Bean Goose *Anser fabalis*

Winter Visitor: A highly localized winter visitor to two areas of Britain, it is a vagrant elsewhere, or at best a passage migrant. It is generally regarded as a sub-species of the pink-footed goose, but is quite distinct in the field. Large numbers winter in Holland and eventually these may overspill to Britain.

Habitat: Damp meadows and other grassland areas.

Locations: Now regular in January and February only on the grassy fields at the southern end of Loch Ken, and on the Yare Marshes in Norfolk. The Scottish birds regularly appear at a group of high level waters in the border country in February; Grindon, Greenlee, Broomlee and Crag Loughs are worth inspecting at this time.

Pink-footed Goose *Anser brachyrhynchus*

Winter Visitor: All of the pinkfeet of eastern Greenland and Iceland come to Britain in winter. They arrive early in October and then gather at several traditional haunts before spreading out over the country. Numbers at such times may be quite staggering, though throughout their stay pinkfeet maintain the largest of goose flocks. The total population of 75,000 makes the species the most numerous goose in Britain.

Habitat: Tundra, glacial deltas; outside breeding season it frequents arable land resorting to estuaries or large inland waters to roost.

Locations: Loch Leven is the major autumn arrival point; largest winter concentrations at Loch Leven 10,000; Loch Balgavies and Loch Rescobie 2,500; Carsebreck Curling Ponds 6,000; Tay Estuary 5,000; Flanders Moss 3,000; Gladhouse 4,000; Cobbinshaw 2,000; Hule Moss 2,000; Caerlaverock 5,000; Rockcliffe 10,000; Ribble 20,000; Humber 1,000; and The Wash. Additionally there are a number of smaller resorts such as the Loch of Strathbeg, which is a good autumn arrival point, and many other lochs in central and eastern Scotland.

White-fronted Goose *Anser albifrons*

Winter Visitor: There are two sub-species of white-fronted geese that find a winter refuge in Britain: the European whitefront *A.a. albifrons* winters in Holland with about 6,000 continuing on to southern England and Wales in October and staying to mid-March. The Greenland whitefront *A.a. flavirostris* numbers 4,500 and winters in Scotland and Wales where they arrive in October and stay to mid-April.

Habitat: Grasslands, preferably wet and splashy; roosts on large lakes nearby.

Locations: Greenland whitefronts frequent many of the areas favoured by barnacle geese in the west of Scotland: South Uist; Tiree at The Reef; Islay about 1,200; Kintyre at Campbeltown and on the shore opposite Gigha; Loch Ken. Also at Anglesey and Tregaron 500.

European whitefronts are less scattered; large numbers can only be found at Slimbridge 5,000; Avon Floods 1,000; North Kent 1,000; Swale 1,000; Towy Valley 1,000.

Lesser White-fronted Goose
Anser erythropus

Vagrant: A smaller edition of the white-fronted goose, but with a larger white frontal shield and conspicuous yellow eye ring. Its habit of appearing in the company of flocks of other geese, often several thousand strong, makes searching a tedious and time-consuming business. Essentially an eastern European bird that occurs once or twice each year.
Habitat: Grasslands, usually splashy.
Locations: Though it has occurred singly in a number of places there are only two regular resorts. Most winters, between December and March, birds are noted at Slimbridge among the flocks of white-fronted geese, and/or on the Yare Marshes among the small flock of bean geese.

Greylag Goose *Anser anser*

Resident: Between 100 and 200 pairs of native greylags breed in the extreme north-west of Scotland, particularly in the Outer Hebrides. Elsewhere there are small, but growing populations of feral birds in southern Scotland in Galloway and Dumfries, in the Lake District, in East Anglia, and in the Midlands and Kent.
Habitat: Marshes and swamps in summer, undisturbed waters with adjacent grassland and arable land in winter.
Locations: Loch Druidibeg NNR on South Uist has about 70 pairs which can easily be seen from public roads and which constitute over half of the native population. Feral populations at Lochinch, Wigtownshire (now controlled at about 500 birds); Duddon Estuary,

Cumbria; north Norfolk and the Broads as at Barton Broad; Tring Reservoirs, Hertfordshire.

Winter Visitor: Over 60,000 of the Icelandic population arrive from mid-October and stay through to mid-April. Most venture no farther than Scotland, with particularly heavy concentrations in the eastern lowlands. A small population comes as far south as Morecambe Bay. Flocks are generally medium-sized with a diurnal routine of feeding on grassland, barley stubbles and potato fields, moving off to a favoured loch to roost.

Locations: Lake of Mentieth; Loch Ken; Cameron Reservoir; Kilconquhar Loch; Loch of Strathbeg; Ythan Estuary; Moray Firth; Cromarty Firth; Loch Leven; Loch of Lintrathen, Loch Rescobie and Loch Balgavies; Montrose Basin; Tay Estuary.

Snow Goose *Anser caerulescens*

Vagrant: Formerly divided into greater and lesser snow geese, and before that into snow and blue geese, all snow geese are now regarded by taxonomists as belonging to the single species. However, the point is made – snow geese vary considerably in size and colouring. They breed in Canada and migrate through the United States to winter. Some occur in Britain every year and may well get mixed up with the Greenland whitefronts that make the trans-Atlantic journey every autumn. However, so many snow geese escape from captivity that all records are suspect.

Habitat: Tundra marshes; in winter frequents marshes and grasslands, often near coast.

Locations: Most frequently observed in October and November and most often in Scotland in company with other geese. No favoured spots in Britain.

Canada Goose *Branta canadensis*

Resident: Introduced in Britain in the seventeenth century, the Canada goose has spread and prospered and now numbers 20,000 birds. In its native North America it is gregarious and highly migratory. Unfortunately in transferring across the Atlantic it has lost both traits and one is most likely to find an isolated pair on a small stretch of water with islands. However, some large flocks do occur.

Habitat: Ponds and lakes with islands; some movement to gather at moulting grounds; at times it resorts to estuarine marshes.

Locations: Largest concentration is at Holkham, but other parts of Norfolk, the Midlands, Harewood and Eccup in Yorkshire, the London parks, Ellesmere and the other Shropshire meres have good numbers. Birds are decidedly scarce in Scotland. A few 'small' Canada geese have been tentatively identified as the cackling Canada goose and are regarded as wild vagrants from America to the Hebrides.

Barnacle Goose *Branta leucopsis*

Winter Visitor: The barnacle geese of Britain come from two quite distinct populations. The Spitzbergen population winters on the Scottish Solway, while the population of east Greenland finds refuge in the Hebrides, with some birds going further west to winter in Ireland. It is an attractive black, white and grey goose confusable only with the brent, but easily distinguished. Once heavily over-shot, protection has restored its numbers.

Habitat: Tundra, usually near the sea; in winter frequents moist grasslands near sea and saltings.

Locations: The 3,000-plus strong Spitzbergen population winters at Caerlaverock from the end of September to mid-April. The Greenland population of 25,000 is concentrated on Islay where 20,000 winter. Best numbers are found at Loch Gruinart and the adjacent Ardnave Peninsula from late October to mid-April. Smaller though significant flocks are found in the Outer Hebrides at Loch Bee on South Uist; otherwise the geese frequent uninhabited islands throughout the Hebrides. Elsewhere, the occasional barnacle appears with other geese at coastal sites, though the likelihood of an escape cannot be ignored.

Brent Goose *Branta bernicla*

Winter Visitor: Two distinct sub-species of brent geese are found in

Britain. The dark-bellied *B.b. bernicla* now numbers up to 40,000 spread around the coasts of the south-east from The Wash to south Devon. The light-bellied *B.b. hrota* winters mainly in Denmark with a regular overspill of about 1,000 coming to the north-east of England. Elsewhere in the country these birds are rare. They spend their time in large flocks throughout their stay.

Habitat: Tundra; estuaries and other inter-tidal areas with strong growth of eel grass, and nearby pastures.

Locations: A string of outstanding haunts in the south-east is home to flocks of brent from November through to late March. Wells 6,000; Blackwater 5,000; Colne 1,000; Dengie 2,500; Foulness 10,000; Hamford 2,500; Leigh 5,000; Crouch 500; Stour 500; Medway 1,000; Swale 2,500; Chichester 10,000; Pagham 250; Keyhaven 500; Langstone 5,000; Newtown 500; Poole 250; Chesil 250; Exe 1,000. Most of these locations are easily accessible except for Foulness which is completely out of bounds.

Egyptian Goose *Alopochen aegyptiacus*

Resident: Introduced in England in the eighteenth century it has recently been accorded a place on the British List as a self-supporting population. A widespread African species that lives mainly in pairs and perches freely in trees. It formerly bred along the Danube.

Habitat: Inland waters and marshes, river banks; in Britain on ornamental lakes and nearby marshes.

Locations: Only reliable spots are Holkham Hall park and adjacent marshes at several spots in the Broads, and in the Brecks.

Shelduck *Tadorna tadorna*

Resident: An attractive duck that is widespread along coasts of north-western Europe, but which also inhabits large areas of central Asia. It gathers in large numbers to moult, but is otherwise found in small flocks. Most British birds migrate to the Heligoland Bight to moult from June to October or even November, but some 4,000 make for Bridgwater Bay.

Habitat: Dunes, plantations near the sea, estuaries, open shores, marshes; seldom more than a couple of miles from the shoreline in either direction.

Locations: Breeds on most shorelines of Britain, though is most numerous on shallow shores such as those in East Anglia. Large numbers can be found at Bridgwater Bay in late summer and autumn; and at other times at Exe, Kingsbridge, Poole Harbour, Langstone, Chichester 5,000, Pagham, Swale 2,500, Medway, Thames, Leigh Marshes, Crouch, Stour 2,500, Hamford Water, Foulness, Dengie, Colne, Blackwater, Breydon, Wash, Lindisfarne, Morecambe Bay, Dee, Mersey, Burry Inlet, Montrose Basin, Eden 1,000.

Mandarin Duck *Aix galericulata*

Resident: Deliberate introductions and escapes have created a feral population of mandarins in Britain. As a 'natural' bird it is confined to the Pacific, USSR and Japan with movement southwards to winter in China. In Britain it is a resident, with a population probably in excess of 1,000 birds.

Habitat: Small lakes and dams surrounded by undisturbed wooded country, a habitat that is far from common in Britain.

Locations: About four fifths of the population can be found in Surrey and Berkshire, but there are also birds in Sussex, on secluded 'hammer' ponds for example, in Norfolk, at Eaton Hall in Cheshire, on the Isle of Wight and at Holmwood in Perthshire. The best places are usually in or near areas where they first escaped: Virginia Water and Windsor Great Park, Cobham, and the River Mole south of Esher are the most reliable.

Wigeon *Anas penelope*

Resident: A scarce breeding bird over most of Britain, the wigeon is largely confined to upland districts of England and Scotland, though it is said to be the most numerous breeding duck in Caithness and has its greatest concentration on the low-lying Loch Leven. Estimates vary from 300 to 500 pairs annually, of which those south of the Pennines are at best sporadic.

Habitat: Inland waters with low-lying islands, but also coastal marshes. In winter frequents saltings and wet grazing.

Locations: Northern Pennines, Scottish Highlands, Orkney but not Shetland.

Winter Visitor: Huge numbers, perhaps 200,000, arrive from Scandinavia and northern Russia to winter in Britain. Some also come from Iceland. They form dense flocks and the majority are coastal, though the largest population of all is found inland.

Locations: Perhaps 35,000 on the Ouse Washes between November and January. Other large concentrations at Dornoch Firth, 5,000 up to 10,000 in autumn; Cromarty Firth 10,000; Montrose Basin; Eden 1,000; Lindisfarne 10,000; Humber, Derwent Floods 5,000; Wash 10,000; Stour 5,000; Dengie 2,500; Blackwater 3,000; Abberton 5,000; North Kent 1,000; Medway 10,000; Swale 5,000; Ribble 5,000; Wigtown Bay. Several other places have flocks in excess of 1,000 birds throughout the winter.

Gadwall *Anas strepera*

Resident: Widespread and numerous in Russia, the gadwall has a patchy distribution throughout the whole of the rest of Europe. It is a partial migrant with birds nesting east of a line drawn from Holland to Greece and moving southwards and westwards. Thus our own birds are augmented by winter visitors from Iceland and northern Europe. It is a delicately-marked species that may easily be confused with mallard at a distance.

Habitat: Lowland waters; marshes, lakes and reservoir edges, slowly-flowing waters.

Locations: East Anglia is the most regular and densely populated region with the largest numbers concentrated on the Breckland lakes where the initial introduction in 1850 took place: River Lark, Narford Lake, Micklemere, Fowlmere, Livermere. Other good spots are Cley, Minsmere 40 pairs, Walberswick, Ouse Washes 25 pairs, Grafham, Havergate, Stodmarsh and North Kent. Other populations exist in the south-west centred on Chew 20 pairs; the north-west at Leighton Moss and Martin Mere; and eastern Scotland centred on Loch Leven 25 pairs. Total about 250 pairs.

Last of the summer visitors to arrive, the **marsh warbler** is a scarce and highly localised breeding bird. About three-quarters of the total population can be found in Worcestershire.

Top The delightful **red-necked phalarope** breeds at a few scattered localities in the Outer Isles and Shetland, but is best seen on autumn passage when it may be storm-driven inland.

Bottom Common enough in appropriate marshland habitat, the **water rail** is frequently heard but seldom seen. The only reasonable way to see one is to frequent marshes, listen for its strange calls, and trust to luck.

Teal *Anas crecca*

Resident: Some 3,500 to 6,000 pairs of teal breed in Britain, the majority in the north, but the rest scattered throughout the country. These numbers are swamped by some 60,000 winter visitors amounting, at times, to about half the total European population in December or January. They are gregarious and often form dense flocks that, like some species of waders, perform complex aerial evolutions. Some gatherings are truly enormous.

Habitat: Large inland waters, swampy grasslands, reservoirs, estuaries and shorelines, marshes.

Locations: Marshes in many parts of the country have a few pairs of teal, but it is only in the northern part of the country that large numbers breed.

Winter Visitor: The winter influx of teal stems from Scandinavia, Russia and Poland and brings birds to almost every part of Britain. Every sizeable lowland reservoir, every estuary and every marsh receives its quota, but some places remain outstanding.

Locations: Martin Mere 10,000; Ouse Washes 5,000; Medway 5,000; Ribble 2,500; Abberton 1,000; Leighton Moss 1,000; Dee 1,000; Rostherne 1,000; Blagdon 1,000; Poole 1,000; Crouch 1,000; Slimbridge 1,000; Fawley 1,000; Langstone 1,000; Humber 1,000; Hickling 1,000; Blithfield 1,000; Minsmere 1,000; Cley 1,000; Derwent Floods; Cromarty 1,000; Dornoch 1,000; Tay 1,000.

Mallard *Anas platyrhynchos*

Resident: Mallard are the most numerous and widespread of British duck, breeding in every county and virtually every parish in the country. The resident birds are augmented by an influx of continental migrants in autumn and peak numbers 'guesstimated' at 300,000 can then be found. These are spread widely over a number of waters, though some large concentrations do occur.

Habitat: Marshes, lakes, ponds, reservoirs, rivers, parks, canals, floods.

Locations: Breeding birds in every part of Britain save a few high mountain massifs.

Winter Visitor: Large influx from the continent of Europe most obvious in the eastern part of the country.
Locations: Large flocks at: Loch of Lintrathen 5,000; Martin Mere 5,000; Abberton 5,000; Ouse Washes 5,000; Tay 2,500; Loch Leven 2,500; Kilconquhar Loch 2,500; Hornsea 2,500; Humber 5,000; Slimbridge 2,500; Dengie 2,500; Dee 2,500; Rostherne 2,500; Grafham 2,500; Blithfield 2,500; Bridgewater 2,500; Hickling 2,500; Wash 2,500; Eyebrook 2,500; Ribble 2,500.

Pintail *Anas acuta*

Resident: Probably less than 50 pairs of pintail breed every year. It is thus one of the rarest British breeding ducks. Reports tend to be scattered through the country and breeding can be considered regular at only a handful of locations. It has a circumpolar distribution and about half of the winter population of Europe, mainly drawn from northern Russia, resorts to Britain at this time. There is also some onward movement to Iberia. Pintail are gregarious birds that form a few large flocks and are generally absent elsewhere.
Habitat: Marshes; flooded grasslands, reservoir margins, estuaries.
Locations: Breeding is annual only in Orkney, Thames, Swale, the Ouse Washes and at Millom in Cumbria (feral).
Winter Visitor: About 24,000 pintail winter in Britain and though they can be seen in small numbers at places such as Cley and Minsmere, they are concentrated in big numbers elsewhere.
Locations: Dee 5,000; Ouse Washes 2,500; Martin Mere 2,500; Ribble 2,500; Medway 1,000.

Garganey *Anas querquedula*

Summer Visitor: The garganey is a summer visitor to Europe, Russia and central and eastern Asia that leaves its breeding range completely to winter in Africa immediately south of the Sahara and in India and South-east Asia. It arrives in mid-March and departs in mid-October, but in February and December birds occur with some regularity. It breeds as far north as the head of the Gulf of Bothnia and there is some migration through Britain as well as breeding in southern and eastern England.

Habitat: Fresh water marshes and floods, coastal marshes, reservoir and lake margins.

Locations: The breeding at temporarily suitable sites rather than at established locations makes the pin-pointing of garganey exceptionally fraught. The breeding population is probably 50 to 100 pairs. The Ouse Washes is a favoured spot and Stodmarsh regularly gets the first of the summer visitors. North Kent, Sandwich Bay, Dungeness, Rye Harbour, Pevensey are all good spots in the south. And there is generally a pair or two along the North Norfolk coast, Cley being a favourite spot. Further north Hornsea may have a pair as may Fairburn Ings.

Shoveler *Anas clypeata*

Summer Visitor: A widespread but uncommon breeding bird over most of Britain, and more or less absent from the west and the Highlands. About 1,000 pairs arrive in spring from their wintering grounds in France, Spain and Portugal, while at the same time a winter population of continental immigrants departs eastward. This is an attractive, easily identified species that has very definite food requirements.

Habitat: Marshes and floods with plentiful emergent vegetation and mud.

Locations: Though it breeds anywhere from the Orkneys to the Isles of Scilly, there are few really reliable spots to find the shoveler in summer. The Ouse Washes is the most significant spot, with perhaps 20 per cent of the British total, followed by the North Kent Marshes, Minsmere, Derwent Floods, Norfolk Broads.

Winter Visitors: About 5,000 birds winter in Britain and concentrations occur in several parts of the country.

Locations: Leighton Moss 500; Loch Leven 500; Abberton 500; Chew 500; The Wash 500; Hickling 500; Blagdon 250; Rostherne 250; Hanningfield 250; Slimbridge 250; Tring 250; Humber 250; Medway 250; North Kent 250; Stodmarsh 250; Minsmere 250.

Red-crested Pochard *Netta rufina*

Passage Migrant: Though red-crested pochard breed in small numbers in Britain every year, and regularly at Frampton-on-Severn, they are not, as yet, considered to have established themselves as a fully self-supporting feral population. Genuinely wild birds occur each autumn on or near the east coast, though there are invariably some escapes as well.

Habitat: Fresh water marshes, shallow lagoons and lakes with emergent vegetation, large reservoirs.

Locations: A regular flock of varying numbers at Abberton is regarded as consisting mainly of wild birds dispersing from Holland; August to October.

Pochard *Aythya ferina*

Resident: Some 200 to 400 pairs of pochard breed in Britain and there is some evidence of a recent increase. Doubtless this process has been aided by the numerous escapes establishing feral flocks, particularly in the south and east of the country.

Habitat: Lakes and pools surrounded by emergent vegetation; in winter frequents gravel pits and reservoirs.

Locations: Southern and eastern England have most breeding records and there are genuinely wild birds on many park ponds and lakes. Scotland and Wales have smaller populations, and it is completely absent from Devon, Cornwall and Shetland.

Winter Visitor: Large numbers of winter visitors arrive in October from eastern Europe and western Russia. They are spread through the country with some quite remarkable concentrations; total population about 45,000.

Locations: Duddingston Loch 10,000; Ouse Washes 2,500; Cotswold Water Park 2,500; Loch of Harray 2,500; Abberton 1,000; Hornsea 1,000; Thames 1,000; Barn Elms 1,000; Walthamstow 1,000; Cheddar 1,000; Kilconquhar Loch 1,000; Strathbeg 1,000; Castle Semple Loch 1,000; Loch Leven 1,000.

Tufted Duck *Aythya fuligula*

Resident: The breeding distribution of the tufted duck is remarkably similar to that of the pochard, though there may be ten to fifteen times as many pairs. The greatest concentration is in the south and east with areas of scarceness in the Highlands, Wales and the south-west. During the present century it has increased and spread remarkably, and the total of 4,000 – 5,000 pairs makes it one of the most abundant of British breeding duck.

Habitat: Lakes, reservoirs, ponds, park lakes and gravel pits.

Locations: Avoids the west and the north, otherwise most suitable waters are occupied. Largest breeding numbers at St. Serf's Island, Loch Leven.

Winter Visitor: Large influx from the Continent from October through to February bringing total British population up to 45,000. Many large flocks on reservoirs with some also taking to the sea.

Locations: Loch Harray 3,000; Loch Leven 2,500; Grafham 2,500; Abberton 2,500; Hanningfield 1,000; Cotswold Water Park 1,000; Barn Elms 1,000; Walthamstow 1,000; Queen Mary 1,000; Strathbeg 1,000; Castle Semple Loch 1,000.

Scaup *Aythya marila*

Resident: No more than a handful of pairs of this northern species breed in Britain each year. All have been in the far north with Orkney and the Outer Hebrides proving most favoured in turn. Occasional birds in south and one laid eggs for several years at Havergate though, as she lacked a mate, they were infertile.

Habitat: Large sheets of water in tundra and boreal zone, preferably with islands; in winter resorts to sea coasts and estuaries.

Locations: Papa Westray in Orkney was a regular breeding-ground some years ago, and Balranald in North Uist had the only recent Hebridean record.

Winter Visitor: About 20,000 scaup winter in Britain with small numbers regularly dotted around the coast, the occasional individual or small group inland on a reservoir, and really substantial flocks at a few favoured estuaries.

Locations: Firth of Forth (Musselburgh-Leith) 10,000–20,000; Loch Indaal 2,500; Rough Firth 500; Loch of Harray 250; Dornoch 250; Humber; Snettisham; North Kent; Dee.

Eider *Somateria mollissima*

Resident: A common and quite numerous breeding bird around the coasts of Scotland extending southwards along the east coast of England and on the west coast to one notable site. This is essentially a seaduck that is gregarious throughout the year and gathers into large breeding colonies that are 'farmed' for eiderdown in Iceland and elsewhere.

Habitat: Rocky islets, uninhabited islands, large sand dune systems; outside breeding season offshore over large mussel-beds and thus tends to favour rocky shorelines.

Locations: Breeding locations at many places particularly in northern and western Scotland. Shetland and Orkney have large, though scattered, numbers and there are really large concentrations at the Sands of Forvie and the Farnes. Walney has a well-established colony.

Winter Visitor: Though there is some evidence of an influx of continental birds to east and south-east England, the birds that visit most of our coasts in winter are dispersing from their Scottish breeding haunts.

Locations: There are huge numbers at Leith in the Forth and at the mouth of the Tay but birds extend to all coasts with good numbers at Farnes, Lindisfarne, Snettisham, Blackwater, Colne and the Dengie Flats area. Top Scottish locations are: Leith 10,000; Ythan 2,500; Islay 1,000; Montrose Basin 1,000; Gullane 1,000; Aberlady 500; Eden 500.

King Eider *Somateria spectabilis*

Vagrant: Now reported virtually every year in Britain indicating a considerable recent increase. Breeds in arctic Russia and a considerable number of birds then move westwards to winter along the coasts of Norway as far south as Trondheim and also off eastern Iceland – the latter presumably originating from Greenland. Most records are of males, the females being confused with female eiders.

Habitat: Tundra often well inland: winters along ice-free coasts.

Locations: Though reported from a number of northern coasts, well over half the British records come from Shetland, where birds are increasingly spending the summer. The huge 'voes' of the north-east are particularly favoured.

Steller's Eider *Polysticta stelleri*

Vagrant: An arctic bird that creeps into Europe mostly as a non-breeder only in the Varanger Fjord in Norway, and is a vagrant elsewhere. Breeds on either side of the Bering Sea eastwards to central northern Siberia.
Habitat: Sea coasts and along edge of pack ice outside breeding season; tundra nester.
Locations: The few British records feature birds seen offshore in the north-east of England and (mostly) Scotland, with a strong preponderance in the Outer Hebrides and Shetland.

Long-tailed Duck *Clangula hyemalis*

Winter Visitor: Has almost certainly bred in Shetland and Orkney; otherwise a scarce winter visitor that may be more frequent out of sight of land. Total population perhaps 4,000, with only a few regular flocks of any size. Rare at large inland waters.
Habitat: Lakes and marshes; almost exclusively marine outside the breeding season.
Locations: Found in small numbers at several places on all Scottish coasts, most frequently in the north and east. In England is regular only on east coast: Hamford Water; The Wash; Cley; Lindisfarne 250; Forth, Leith to Musselburgh 250; Aberlady; Gullane Bay; Spey Mouth 100; Ythan; Eden; Dornoch; Dunnet Head; Broad Bay, Lewis; Loch Indaal.

Common Scoter *Melanitta nigra*

Resident: About 30 to 40 pairs of scoter breed in Scotland every year. They are confined to the north and the west where conditions most nearly approximate to their arctic habitat. Proved to breed in 1855, there is evidence of a slow spread and gradual increase since. They are now regular at a handful of sites. There is a large influx in winter.
Habitat: Large bare waters with islands and heather-lined banks; outside breeding season marine usually close to shore, but also quite frequently well out to sea.

Locations: Shetland – Mainland and Yell; southern Caithness – the stronghold; Inverness – where one loch holds half a dozen pairs; Loch Lomond.

Winter Visitor: The influx of 35,000 winter visitors does not include large numbers found out of sight of land. In late summer (July) there is also a considerable movement to our coasts of birds congregating to moult.

Locations: Moult gatherings: Dunwich; Wigtown; Eden. Winter: Eden 5,000; Forth 3,500; Southerness thousands; Wash 2,500; Lindisfarne 1,000; Rye Harbour 250; Foulness; Blakeney-Cley; Dee.

Surf Scoter *Melanitta perspicillata*

Vagrant: This North American sea duck crosses the Atlantic fairly regularly, though almost all accepted records are of the distinctive males. Females are presumably confused with female common and velvet scoters and thus overlooked. Despite their common origin there is neither a pattern in date of occurrence (there being a scattering of records throughout the year), nor in geographical location.

Habitat: Ponds and lakes in northern boreal or tundra zone; winters at sea but close inshore.

Locations: No pattern emerges save that sometimes birds stay on for quite lengthy periods, as for instance on the Scottish Solway from 1964 to 1966 when up to four were present together.

Velvet Scoter *Melanitta fusca*

Winter Visitor: Though the velvet scoter has bred in Scotland, this is exceptional. Birds are, however, present around our coasts all year round with maximum numbers, perhaps up to 5,000, in autumn and winter. With a few exceptions large flocks are unusual and most birds are seen in company with larger numbers of common scoters. They can be picked out, even at a considerable distance, by the white in the wing as they fly.

Habitat: Lakes in predominantly wooded country, tundra, offshore islets; in winter sea coasts, feeding in shallower water than common scoter.

Locations: Eden; Firth of Forth; Snettisham; Cley; Dunwich; Orford-ness; Portland. Small numbers elsewhere.

Goldeneye *Bucephala clangula*

Resident: A small number of goldeneye breed in Britain every year with a total population of less than 20 pairs. These are concentrated in the Scottish Highlands, the Lake District and Gwynedd, though at none of these are the birds particularly visible.

Habitat: Lakes and lochs, sometimes at some altitude; at other seasons on large reservoirs and along coasts.

Locations: Only Speyside and adjacent areas of Inverness offer any real chance of finding breeding goldeneye in Britain.

Winter Visitor: Over 12,000 goldeneye arrive in Britain in October and stay through to March each year. Most come from or through Scandinavia and then spread out unevenly through the country with largest numbers in the north and east.

Locations: Scotland is particularly favoured but good spots in the south include Abberton (top English spot); Grafham; Dee; Rostherne; Hayle; Exe; Kingsbridge; Tamar; Portland; Poole; Hickling; Cley; Blithfield; Breydon; Blackwater; Colne; Hanningfield; Stour; Langstone; Hornsea; Medway; Eyebrook; Wash; William Girling; King George V; Queen Mary. Traeth Bach is a good spot in Wales. Top concentration north of the border is on the Forth at Leith where up to 10,000 may winter over the ·famed mussel beds.

Smew *Mergus albellus*

Winter Visitor: No more than 150 smew come to Britain to winter in the southern and eastern part of the country. They are remarkably conservative in their choice of habitat and return to the same inland water year after year. They breed in the high arctic and feed mostly on fish in winter.

Habitat: Tundra lakes and pools; in winter mainly on rich inland waters particularly, in Britain, lowland reservoirs.

Locations: The London area has long been favoured by wintering smew and birds are present from October to March at Stoke

Newington, Barn Elms and Staines. Elsewhere Virginia Water, Abberton and Chew are regularly favoured.

Red-breasted Merganser *Mergus serrator*

Resident: As a breeding bird the merganser is confined to the north and
west inhabiting the hilly and mountain districts of Scotland, the Lake
District, North Wales and a few spots in the Pennines. In all some 2,000
pairs breed and, though they are joined by some visitors from Iceland
and Scandinavia, it is mainly the British population that spreads
through the country to winter.
Habitat: Mostly sea lochs with islets, though inland along rivers and
lochs. Outside the breeding season is mostly found close inshore and in
estuaries. Inland it is rare even on the largest waters.
Locations: Anglesey and adjacent North Wales, the major lakes of the
Lake District, at many spots in the border country and throughout the
Highlands and Islands.
Winter Visitor: Spreads to most coasts of Britain in small numbers
between October and March.
Locations: Largest concentrations are north of the border at Leith,
Musselburgh, Gullane and other spots on the Forth; Dornoch; Fleet;
Stenness, Cromarty, Moray and Beauly, Ythan.

Goosander *Mergus merganser*

Resident: Much less inclined to the sea than their close relative the red-
breasted merganser, goosanders are not as numerous either as breeding
or wintering birds. They are confined to the Highlands and border
country of Scotland and the adjacent areas of the Lake District and the
Pennines. Nowhere are they common and the total population is no
more than 2,000 pairs.
Habitat: Lakes and large rivers, but up in the hills on quite small streams
and lochs; at other seasons frequents lowland lochs and reservoirs.
Locations: Greatest breeding density extends from the hills north of the
Solway eastwards through the border hills where virtually every river
and large loch is occupied.

Winter Visitor: Some influx from Scandinavia, though total population estimate of 4,000 individuals must be too low.

Locations: Largest concentration is on the Inner Moray Firth. Elsewhere there are small numbers at many waters as, for example, in the London area at William Girling, King George V, Queen Mary; and at Hornsea, Abberton, and the Midland reservoirs, e.g. Grafham, Eyebrook, Pitsford, etc.

Ruddy Duck *Oxyura jamaicensis*

Resident: Introduced accidentally via the Wildfowl Trust's Slimbridge collection, the ruddy duck first bred in 1960 and was admitted to the British List in 1971. After becoming established nearby they soon spread to the West Midlands where they prospered.

Habitat: Reed-fringed meres and other small pools in summer; resorts to larger waters in winter.

Locations: Meres of Cheshire, Salop and Staffordshire – Rostherne, Tatton, Ellesmere, etc. In winter larger reservoirs in Staffordshire, e.g. Blithfield, and at Chew and Blagdon in Avon.

Honey Buzzard *Pernis apivorus*

Summer Visitor: Extremely rare breeding bird with no more than a handful of pairs in southern England each year. Whereabouts are often kept secret even from ornithological authorities. Arrives late in May and best looked for during early June when characteristic 'butterfly' display flight is performed.

Habitat: Woodland, deciduous or mixed, often with surrounding heathland or grassland; such places are particularly scarce in southern England.

Locations: Hampshire is the British headquarters though it has bred further north in the Midlands, the Welsh border country and Norfolk in recent years. Exact locations cannot be given, though some are widely known among bird-watchers.

Passage Migrant: A very scarce bird of passage in spring from mid-May into June and in the autumn from September to mid-October. Nowhere

regular, though one or more in recent years on the well-watched East
Anglian coast. Elsewhere exceptional.
Locations: Norfolk and Suffolk coasts.

Red Kite *Milvus milvus*

Resident: Long confined to a remote district of central Wales, this once
widespread and apparently common bird is still in a vulnerable state.
Some 30 to 35 pairs breed annually, but many desert and the failure rate
is very high. However, numbers are slowly increasing and the birds
have spread away from the Upper Towy valley to occupy areas even
considerable distances away. It is now possible to recommend several
areas where kites may be seen hanging over the valley oak woods.
Habitat: Mainly oak woods along scarps of steep-sided valleys; on
Continent uses wide variety of woodland types.
Locations: The Gwenffrwd and Dinas reserves were established
specifically for the kites and are located at the centre of their
distribution. Nearby is the National Nature Reserve (NNR) of Cors
Tregaron, eastwards from which runs a mountain road, both of which
often produce off-duty birds at all seasons. Red kites can now be looked
for over a huge area: they breed in six counties, and there are even
records for areas in south-west England that could turn into
breeding-grounds.
Vagrant: Elsewhere in Britain the red kite is a very rare vagrant usually
seen briefly where bird-watchers gather.
Locations: None specific.

White-tailed Eagle *Haliaeetus albicilla*

Vagrant: Were it not for the recent attempts to reintroduce this
splendid bird to Britain its status as a very rare vagrant would preclude
its inclusion in this section of the book. Once widespread in Scotland
and the hillier districts of north-western England, the white-tailed eagle
was senselessly persecuted and eventually became extinct in 1916. An
attempted reintroduction at Fair Isle in 1968 failed, but the present
attempt at Rhum seems to be enjoying some success.

Habitat: Sea coasts and cliffs, but also marshes in many parts of its range.

Locations: Isle of Rhum. As a vagrant the white-tailed eagle is too irregular to be located.

Marsh Harrier *Circus aeruginosus*

Resident: A widespread and numerous bird right across the Continent from Portugal to Sakhalin in the Pacific, it includes south-eastern England at the very edge of its range. Despite lavish protection and conservation measures the fortunes of the marsh harrier in Britain continue to fluctuate from apparent imminent doom to encouraging success. A population of 16–17 pairs in 1977 is as healthy a one as we have enjoyed for many years.

Habitat: Marshes, heaths, and large reed beds in which to breed.

Locations: Odd pairs breed in several parts of the country but the only regular spots are all in East Anglia. North Norfolk at Cley, the Broads at Hickling and Horsey and the Suffolk coast at Minsmere are the best sites. It would be an unfortunate visitor to Minsmere who failed to see this bird.

Passage Migrant: Some continental birds pass through and even winter in Britain, though it is difficult to pick them out from our native stock.

Locations: Coastal East Anglia, North Kent at Sheppey.

Hen Harrier *Circus cyaneus*

Resident: This widespread bird breeds right across the northern hemisphere and, depending on one's systematics, may even breed through much of South America. On the continent it is absent from the extreme south, but is found northwards into Lapland. By the turn of the century persecution, as a result of its depredations on young red grouse, had eliminated it everywhere save for Orkney and the Outer Islands where game rearing is of little importance. Careful protection of these stocks enabled a surplus of birds to be produced ready to recolonize the mainland when conditions changed during and after the last war. Now some 300–400 pairs breed from Orkney to Wales and Norfolk and still the spread continues.

Habitat: Moorland and especially young conifer plantations; at other seasons frequents marshes, reed-beds, estuaries.

Locations: Orkney, with 60 + nests, remains the stronghold; try the 'Moors Road' north of Dounby. The hills of Caithness and Sutherland have a good population and there are many among the plantations of Kintyre and Arran eastwards towards Aberdeen, across the southern edge of the Highlands. The border hills have some, as do the Pennines as far south as the North Staffordshire Moors (first breeding 1974). North and central Wales have a growing population and a pair has bred in North Norfolk.

Winter Visitor: Outside the breeding season hen harriers spread southwards or (more likely) arrive from the Continent and can then be found along the east coast bird marshes.

Locations: Cley, Horsey, Yare, Valley, Walberswick, Minsmere, Dengie, Sheppey. Rare in the west.

Montagu's Harrier *Circus pygargus*

Summer Visitor: A graceful, light-flying harrier that has become progressively more scarce in recent years and is now our rarest breeding bird of prey. It is interesting to note that while the Montagu's has declined the hen harrier has spread southward to take its place. The population of this bird has always been cyclical and, being a migrant, recolonization presents few problems.

Habitat: Extensive heaths, but agricultural land in other parts of its range.

Locations: No more than five pairs of these birds have bred in any recent year; usually only one or two. No locations possible.

Passage Migrant: Late April to late September sees a small trickle of birds in various places.

Locations: South and east coast resorts; too few individuals involved to be specific.

Goshawk *Accipiter gentilis*

Resident: A decade ago it was only possible to talk in the vaguest of terms about the status of the goshawk as a British bird. 'Has bred from time to time in Sussex' was about as precise a statement as could have been expected. Today all that has changed, although quite why it is difficult to see. Falconers' birds, often complete with jesses, have escaped in many parts of the country, found each other and settled down to breed in a feral existence. Today there are some 19 known pairs, with others still being kept secret, from the Cairngorms to Sussex.

Habitat: Large and dense deciduous, coniferous or mixed forests.

Locations: Best looked for during March and April when it displays high over its territory. Southern Scotland and north Midlands seem to have the highest numbers, but no specific locations possible.

Sparrowhawk *Accipiter nisus*

Resident: Breeds right across Eurasia as well as southwards into North Africa and the Himalayas. It is a summer visitor to much of this area, but in Britain birds are resident, though augmented by winter visitors from the Continent that arrive in September. During the terrible pesticide period of the 1950s and 1960s the population of this active, fast-flying hawk was decimated and it became extinct in many areas. Only the effective campaigning by ornithologists and the subsequent ban on the use of chlorinated hydrocarbons saved the sparrowhawk. Today it is back in many of its old haunts with a population of perhaps 15,000 pairs.

Habitat: Woodland of all types; also hedgerows, copses and agricultural land with woodland nearby.

Locations: Absent from the fens, from London and the other great urban conglomerations, from the treeless highlands of the Pennines and Scotland and from large areas of Kent and Suffolk. Otherwise to be looked for everywhere. Behaviour, especially wheeling flight with soaring interspersed by bouts of wing flapping, distinguishes it from the kestrel.

Winter Visitor: Difficult to distinguish from resident population, but more plentiful along east coast at this time.

Common Buzzard *Buteo buteo*

Resident: Though the population of common buzzards in Britain was seriously reduced by indiscriminate slaughter in the nineteenth century, sufficient numbers remained for the population to build up very quickly when conditions improved during and after the last war. The 12,000 pairs recorded in 1954 represented the highest population since at least the early part of last century, but then myxamatosis struck. The rabbit population was decimated and with it went the common buzzard's staple food. The birds simply disappeared from many areas and became once more confined to the hilly districts of the country. These populations suffered during the pesticide dramas of the 1960's when chlorinated hydrocarbons were widely used in sheep dips and when, in the absence of rabbits, buzzards turned their attentions to sheep carrion. The revival of the rabbit has led to another increase in buzzards with perhaps 10,000 pairs in the country.

Habitat: Hilly wooded districts, but also lowland woods if sufficiently undisturbed.

Locations: Huge populations of buzzards in Wales and Devon make it almost impossible to visit those areas without seeing birds soaring overhead. Cornwall, the New Forest and Dorset, Lake District, the southern hills of Scotland and the entire Highland region are all good buzzard areas.

Winter Visitor: Continental visitors frequent the east coast marshes in small numbers most winters.

Rough-legged Buzzard *Buteo lagopus*

Winter Visitor: Like so many arctic breeding birds, the population of rough-legged buzzards tends to be cyclical and intimately connected to the population of small arctic rodents, especially lemmings. A crash in the small mammal population may leave huge numbers of predators high and dry with a resulting dispersal in their desperate search for food. Rough-legged buzzards arrive on the east coast every October, but some years there may be a veritable invasion.

Habitat: Arctic tundra, with or without trees and shrubs; in winter frequents coastal marshes and seldom ventures inland.

Locations: The whole east coast from Scotland to Kent has regular rough-legged haunts. Best sites are Spurn, Cley, Walberswick and Sheppey.

Golden Eagle *Aquila chrysaetos*

Resident: Despite everything that man has done to destroy it, the golden eagle survives and may indeed prosper in the Highlands of Scotland. Shot for its depredations on red grouse, poisoned by feeding on sheep carrion, robbed of its eggs by collectors, disturbed by photographers and over-zealous bird-watchers – still the golden eagle maintains a population of about 250 pairs. It is the only huge soaring bird in Britain and its prominent head in flight distinguishes it easily from the buzzard. In 1969 a pair nested in England in the Lake District for the first time this century: it would be best if they were left in peace – there are plenty that are easier to see north of the border. This eagle has a huge circumpolar distribution, though there are few places where it could be regarded as common.

Habitat: Moorlands with cliffs or forests, also occasionally sea cliffs.
Locations: Though there are several sites in the border hills, especially in the west toward Galloway, the would-be eagle-watcher would be best advised to concentrate his attention on the Highlands and the Inner and Outer Hebrides. Within this huge area golden eagles are thinly spread being both highly territorial and resident. The more or less certain locations are all in the far north and west at Inverpolly, Loch Maree, Beinn Eighe, Kylesku and Clo Mor, most of which require a bit of effort to ensure sightings. Watching the hillsides is the key to success.

Osprey *Pandion haliaetus*

Summer Visitor: Very scarce summer visitor. Between 10 and 30 pairs breed regularly in Scotland which was recolonized in the mid-1950s after an absence of 40 years.

Habitat: Though it formerly bred on cliffs, promontories and in ruins, all recent nests have been in trees. It can be looked for throughout the Highlands wherever there are large lochs with a good head of fish and nearby forests or clumps of large trees.

Locations: (1) The RSPB reserve at Loch Garten is open free of charge throughout the season and features a special hide and educational display together with commentary; thousands of visitors every year.

(2) Loch of Lowes is a reserve of the Scottish Wildlife Trust and features the only other freely available ospreys; hide and visitor centre.
Passage Migrant: In spring ospreys pass through Britain with barely a pause from mid-April onwards, in autumn their progress is more leisurely and they are regularly noted off-passage at many large inland waters. The creation of large lowland reservoirs, often stocked with high populations of sport fish, has led to increasing records of autumn ospreys even in the Midlands and south-eastern England. Doubtless the Scottish population is augmented by Scandinavian migrants at this time.
Locations: Large lowland reservoirs and even small fisheries e.g. Rutland Water, Grafham, Eyebrook, Weir Wood.

Kestrel *Falco tinnunculus*

Resident: Perhaps as many as 75,000 pairs of kestrels breed in Britain making this species by far the most common of raptors. There is hardly a region that does not support it and the 'Atlas' discovered a density of 75 pairs per 10 km. square. It is also numerous in other parts of its range which extends from South Africa through Arabia and India to China and Japan as well as throughout Europe. Due mainly to its hovering flight alongside motorways it is now as familiar to the town dweller as it has always been to the countryman. It has even spread into city centres where its normal diet of small mammals has been abandoned in favour of house sparrows.
Habitat: Remarkable variety of niches from rolling agricultural land with copses and hedgerows to city centres, sea cliffs, moorlands and even prairies, provided there are nest sites available.
Locations: Any motorway, and in every part of the country save for the fens where lack of nest sites may be a factor; some parts of the Highlands and Islands and the Shetlands.
Winter Visitor: Continental birds arrive in eastern Scotland and other parts of the east coast, but soon spread out and become indistinguishable from our resident birds.
Locations: None specific.

Red-footed Falcon *Falco vespertinus*

Vagrant: Breeding from the Balkans eastwards, the red-footed falcon is at best a very rare passage migrant in Britain. Most birds recorded in spring with a mid-May peak, but numbers may vary from none to several dozen. Being essentially a gregarious bird, parties of up to 30 or 40 are sometimes recorded on the Continent, though 5 is a large party in Britain. Though it hovers like a kestrel, it most closely resembles a hobby though it has shorter wings and is slightly smaller than the latter. It feeds mainly in the air and is a summer visitor throughout its range.
Habitat: Steppes with woods, forest edges, agricultural land, parklands; on passage in a wide variety of areas.
Locations: Seldom seen before May with spring passage extending through June. Dorset, Hampshire, Kent and Norfolk are prime counties with a surprising number of records in Shetland. The New Forest in mid-May offers the peak chance.

Merlin *Falco columbarius*

Resident: This little falcon of the hills is distributed throughout the hilly districts of Britain, but it is nowhere common and the total British population is no more than 500–600 pairs. It has a circumpolar distribution extending beyond the Arctic Circle and many of these northern birds are migrants southwards to Britain in winter. At this season they frequent coastal marshes along the east coast. Their characteristic method of hunting involves fast low-level attacks on flocks of small birds.
Habitat: Moorlands in upland districts, resorting to coastal marshes and grazing in winter.
Locations: Greatest densities are found in the Pennines and in north and central Wales. The Yorkshire Moors, the border country and the Scottish Highlands all have good numbers as does Exmoor (but not Dartmoor) in the extreme south. Shetland and Orkney are both well populated.
Winter Visitor: South-east of a line from the Severn to the Humber the merlin is only a winter visitor to coasts in small numbers.

Locations: The Wash, North Norfolk, Suffolk, Sheppey and North Kent.

Hobby *Falco subbuteo*

Summer Visitor: About 100 pairs of hobbies arrive in late April to breed in southern England. They are elegant, fast-flying falcons that take their prey in the air feeding mainly on large flying insects, but turn their attention to swallows and martins during the breeding season. With long wings and medium-length tail they resemble kestrels, and even more, red-footed falcons, but they do not hover and they have pronounced dark moustaches like the peregrine. Being right at the northern edge of their range hobbies have probably never been very numerous in Britain, but they have for generations been a favourite prey to egg collectors and doubtless they still are. Certainly much secrecy continues to surround the whereabouts of most hobbies in this country.

Habitat: Heaths and downland with clumps of deciduous or coniferous trees.

Locations: The British headquarters of the hobby extends from Devon to Sussex and northwards to Warwickshire and Bedfordshire. Very few exact sites are publishable, but the New Forest and the Surrey Heaths are noted haunts. Dorset, Wiltshire, Hampshire, Somerset and Surrey contain most pairs. Best looked for in late May and early June when display flight makes them reasonably obvious.

Gyrfalcon *Falco rusticolus*

Vagrant: This magnificent falcon, much in demand by the rich falconers of the Middle East, has undoubtedly declined over large parts of its range which has led, in turn, to a reduction in the number of birds that come to Britain. Its status as a European breeding bird is very much at risk and there can be no doubt that most birds that visit us originate in Canada and Greenland and are of the *candicans* white variety. Icelandic gyrfalcons are grey.

Habitat: Arctic tundra with cliffs and bluffs.

Locations: Its north-western origins brings the gyrfalcon mainly to western Britain and it is most likely to be seen in Shetland, northern Scotland, Devon and Cornwall, and the Isles of Scilly. Most are reported in March, but there is another peak in November-December.

Peregrine *Falco peregrinus*

Resident: A scarce breeding bird that was widespread and quite numerous until the pesticide disaster of the mid-1950s. Thanks almost entirely to the work of ornithologists, the danger of these chemicals was recognised much earlier here than in other countries and, as a result, the peregrine population slumped but was not wiped out. Britain now boasts one of the strongest populations in the world. Unfortunately the international demand for peregrines for falconry has placed a scarcity price on the birds and there is a highly organized network of thieves at work. In the circumstances nesting locations must of necessity be left vague.

Habitat: Cliffs, both inland and along coasts where nests are used over and over again. In winter frequents estuaries, coastal marshes and inland wastelands.

Locations: A very few remain in the south-west, in north Wales, the Lake District and the Scottish border country. By far the largest numbers are confined to the Highlands and Islands of Scotland.

Passage Migrant and **Winter Visitor:** Peregrines arrive from Scandinavia in small numbers every autumn and some pass onwards. Others take up residence along coasts and marshes and often appear quite regularly.

Locations: Many coastal birding areas produce a peregrine every so often but few can be relied upon to produce one year after year. At Slimbridge the species occurs most winters and it can usually be seen along the Essex coast, near Bradwell for instance.

Red Grouse *Lagopus lagopus*

Resident: The famous British red grouse is but a race of the Continental willow grouse, which has a circumpolar breeding distribution, being called the 'willow ptarmigan' in North America. It is totally resident and completely unknown away from its breeding haunts. These, however, are carefully preserved and manage to produce as large a surplus as possible for sport. Thus there can be no doubt that the half million or so pairs is far greater than the 'natural' population.

Habitat: Large open heather moorlands, or grassy moors with extensive stands of heather.

Locations: Dartmoor and Exmoor still have small populations; the Welsh hills have some good moors; the whole of the Pennines as well as the Yorkshire Moors and parts of the Lake District have good populations; the border hills, the whole of the Scottish Highlands, Orkney and the Outer Hebrides all have good grouse moors. A good moor is one that has been managed, a fact that is most easily discerned by the patchwork effect produced by controlled burning. To see red grouse, walk a heather moor, or be about on 12th August when the shooting season opens and birds are 'beaten'.

Ptarmigan *Lagopus mutus*

Resident: A high arctic species that extends southwards to reach Scotland, and beyond that only some of the highest mountains of Europe. In summer its plumage of mottled greys and browns merges perfectly with the broken rocky terrain of Scotland's highest plateaux: in winter its all-white feathers are equally effective among the snowy wastes. It is naturally liable to large population fluctuations depending on the severity of the season, and numbers in autumn may be ten times those in spring. Overall Scotland has a good population of what is always an elusive bird requiring hard walking to locate.

Habitat: High level tundra-type landscape with few, if any, bushes or trees.

Locations: Confined, mainly in the west, to the highest mountains of Scotland from Argyll northwards, but descending to about 1,000 feet in the Cape Wrath region. Highest numbers found in Aberdeenshire, but it is easiest to locate ptarmigan on Cairngorms which can be reached without difficulty via the ski lift. Good numbers also found north of the Caledonian Canal in Wester Ross centred on Torridon. Skye and Mull also have ptarmigan.

Black Grouse *Tetrao tetrix*

Resident: Though a good population of black grouse inhabit Britain, certainly in excess of 10,000 pairs, they are never an easy bird to see without local guidance. They are confined to grassy heather slopes in hilly districts with a good growth of conifers nearby. Their communal leks are established on traditional grounds which they are very loathe to abandon and there are examples of birds returning to display on what has become a building site instead of a meadow. Though they breed in many hilly districts they are certainly more numerous north of the border; indeed the border country seems ideally suited to their needs.

Habitat: Moorland adjacent to forest, with grassy meadows and much heather.

Locations: The small population on Exmoor apparently lacks the ability to maintain itself without artificial introductions and is, indeed, very small. Best areas are found by exploring the minor roads through the hills of Kirkcudbrightshire, Dumfries and Selkirk. North of the lowlands Perthshire is very good: try the B934 south of Dunning. Among the islands only Islay has a really good population, and north of the Caledonian Canal the birds are not nearly as numerous.

Capercaillie *Tetrao urogallus*

Resident: By 1785 the native population of capercaillies had been shot out of existence and our present birds are descendants of Continental birds introduced over a lengthy period but principally in 1837 at Kenmore at the mouth of Loch Tay. Today they are widespread, though not numerous, over much of central eastern Scotland. For such a huge bird they are particularly elusive, though once found they are persistent in the territories they hold.

Habitat: Old forests of Scots pine with heather and berries, but also modern plantations of exotic conifers preferably with an admixture of the native pine.

Locations: The major remnants of the old Caledonian forests including Rothiemurchus, Glenmore, Mar, Balmoral, Culbin and the Black

Wood of Rannoch all hold capercaillies. They are confined in the Scottish lowlands and are not found in the west or north.

Red-legged Partridge *Alectoris rufa*

Resident: First introduced in 1673 the red-legged, or 'French partridge' as it is often known, overlaps in range with the native grey partridge. It does, however, prefer drier areas and is thus more or less confined to the south and east of Britain despite frequent attempts to introduce it elsewhere. It is also more tolerant of agricultural activities than the grey and in many areas is more numerous as a result.

Habitat: Agricultural land, heaths, coverts, downland and even woodland rides.

Locations: Absent from Devon and Cornwall, most of Wales, Lancashire and the Pennines and from the Yorkshire Moors northwards. Otherwise generally spread through south-east England. East Anglia has a particularly strong population.

Grey Partridge *Perdix perdix*

Resident: Though it has declined in numbers seriously enough to worry the game interests for whom it represents a major quarry, the native grey partridge is still widespread in Britain and absent from only the highest upland areas. The reasons for decline are not easily ascertained, but changing agricultural techniques and a series of late springs leading to chick starvation are the usually quoted causes. Elsewhere the species extends eastwards through Europe as far as central Siberia and northern India.

Habitat: Agricultural land with hedgerows and wasteland, heaths, ploughed downland.

Locations: Absent from large areas of Wales and from the Highlands of Scotland, though it is numerous in the lowlands and the eastern part of that country. Absent also from Shetland, Orkney and the Hebrides save for Coll. Elsewhere easily found particularly in autumn when numbers are highest and the fields are bare.

Quail *Coturnix coturnix*

Summer Visitor: Once a numerous and widespread summer visitor to the countryside of Britain, the quail is now rare enough to be missed completely by the bird watcher year after year. It is, of course, an easy bird to overlook and is generally located by its call and/or by flushing it, but the decline is quite real. The reasons are complex, but earlier harvesting of the hay crop and the serious over-shooting of spring migrants in southern Europe are certainly involved.

Habitat: Grassland and waste, agricultural land including hay and cereal crop fields.

Locations: Mostly to be sought from late April to September on the chalk downland (ploughed or not) of southern England: South Downs, North Downs, Wiltshire, Marlborough, the Chilterns, etc. A scattering elsewhere suggests that these birds may still turn up anywhere, though the north of England, Wales and Scotland are not favoured very often.

Reeve's Pheasant *Syrmaticus reevesi*

Resident: Introduced at the tail end of the last century, this very attractive bird has only just managed to establish itself in a feral state and its numbers are regularly augmented by further introductions.

Habitat: Woodlands and fields.

Locations: Most introductions fail eventually, but the birds at Woburn are as consistently present and successful as any. Other current populations are at Elveden in Suffolk and Kinveachy in Inverness.

Pheasant *Phasianus colchicus*

Resident: Apparently introduced after the Norman conquest in the eleventh century, pheasants have naturalized remarkably well in Britain. It is, however, difficult to establish just how successful they would be without the continuous additions to their population provided by the game-rearing industry. Being catholic in their choice of habitat they occupy virtually every corner of Britain save for the highest massifs particularly in northern Scotland. Elsewhere they are numerous with a total population of between 70,000 – 450,000 pairs.

Habitat: Woodlands, fields with hedges and copses, coverts, marshes, parkland, occasionally even moorland.

Locations: Save for the Highlands of Scotland, and some Pennine and Welsh hills, the pheasant can be found in every corner of the country except Shetland, the Outer Hebrides and some of the Inner Hebrides. Its characteristic loud call often attracts attention in woodland areas.

Golden Pheasant *Chrysolophus pictus*

Resident: A native of China, the delightful golden pheasant was introduced into several parts of Britain at the tail end of the last century and has slowly established itself in a feral state and been added to the British List. In two areas it is now regarded as well established and flocks of up to twenty or more are not uncommon. Elsewhere golden pheasants are still being introduced only to breed happily for a season or two, and then die out.

Habitat: Coniferous woods, sometimes mixed forests. In its native China it frequents scrubby hillsides and bamboo thickets.

Locations: The strongest population exists in the Brecks, but another inhabits the Creetown, Kirroughtree, Penninghame area of Galloway. Total population about 500 pairs.

Lady Amherst's Pheasant *Chrysolophus amherstiae*

Resident: This spectacularly beautiful bird was introduced to Britain from about the beginning of the century, though it was not until the 1930s that a viable feral population was established as a result of escapes from Whipsnade and Woburn. Over the years the species has spread and become sufficiently well established to merit a place on the British List.

Habitat: Woodlands with heavy growth of brambles or rhodedendrons.

Locations: Woburn, Whipsnade, Mentmore, Maulden Woods and others in same general area represent the strongholds of this pheasant in Britain. There is also a growing population in the New Forest.

Water Rail *Rallus aquaticus*

Resident: An elusive, easily overlooked bird that enjoys a patchy distribution throughout Britain. It is nowhere numerous, save perhaps for a few east coast reed beds, but is found in all parts of the country except the Highlands and Islands and much of Devon and North Wales. It is most numerous in the south and east. Its weird array of shrieks and calls is easily recognised and very often the only sign of its presence.
Habitat: Reed-beds and other dense marginal marsh vegetation.
Locations: A search, by listening, of large reed beds in any part of Britain may locate a water rail, though a sighting, if obtained at all, is likely to be brief. Excellent spots are Holme, Cley, Hickling, Horsey, Walberswick and Minsmere, all on the east coast, which have as healthy a population as any.

Spotted Crake *Porzana porzana*

Summer Visitor: One of the most elusive of all British birds and virtually impossible to see without flushing – which is dangerous to the birds. It is a summer visitor that inhabits the densest of swamps and is, in any case, far from numerous. However, it is undoubtedly frequently overlooked even though it has a remarkably distinctive call 'quip-quip-quip' that it repeats on and on for hours at a time and which has been likened to a tap continuously dripping into a half empty water cistern.
Habitat: Overgrown swamps, reed beds, sedges and flooded rank grassland.
Locations: Calls are uttered in late May and through June, often not starting until well after dark. The east coast marshes should produce the species, but seldom do so. There are regular spots on the Scottish Solway, but elsewhere this bird is irregular.

Corncrake *Crex crex*

Summer Visitor: Generally present from late April through to the end of September. Once widespread and numerous throughout Britain, and the source of one of the most characteristic of countryside calls, the corncrake has suffered a disastrous decline over the past hundred years. The most likely cause seems to be the ever-increasing level of mechanization of farming which kills the birds and destroys their nests before the chicks hatch or are ready to move. Additionally, these birds are frequently killed by hitting overhead cables while migrating.

Habitat: Grass fields, usually grown for hay; not at all frequent among cereals.

Locations: Usually located by its 'crex-crex' grating call. Still widespread in Britain, but neither numerous nor regular anywhere south of Scotland. Even there it is best searched for among the Islands. Tiree and the western parts of the Outer Hebrides still have large populations that call long into the night. Elsewhere can be looked for in Galloway, Perth, Anglesey and Caernarvon.

Moorhen *Gallinula chloropus*

Resident: Almost a million pairs of moorhens breed in Britain making it by far the most successful member of its family. But the species has also proved very successful elsewhere and has established itself on every continent save for Australia. It is often quite tame and will breed on park and village ponds, and even in the centre of large cities.

Habitat: Ponds, pools, lakes, marshes, gravel pits, reservoirs, canals, but not fast-flowing rivers.

Locations: Every part of Britain except for some hills in Dartmoor, Wales, Pennines and the Highlands of Scotland where it is very localized. Elsewhere can be seen during any day's bird-watching.

Coot *Fulica atra*

Resident: Over most of Europe, the coot is the only all-black, medium-sized waterbird. At sea it could be confused with a scoter, but coots seldom take to salt water. The bold white comb on the forehead is sufficient to separate it from all but the highly localized (in Spain) crested coot.

Habitat: Lakes and ponds, drainage ditches, reed beds, but all with plentiful lush cover. Slow rivers and canals are used to a lesser extent.

Locations: Absent only from some of the hilly districts of the south-west, Wales, Pennines, the Yorkshire Moors and Scotland. Totally absent from large parts of the Highlands, especially north of the Caledonian Canal, and from Shetland and Lewis.

Oystercatcher *Haematopus ostralegus*

Resident: About 30,000 pairs of oystercatchers breed in Britain, almost three-quarters of these in Scotland. Though they nest quite freely inland over a large part of the central Soviet Union, in Britain and other parts of Europe the move inland is comparatively recent. So far this spread has affected Sweden, Holland and adjacent parts of Germany, and Scotland and northern England. At first the move was confined to shingle banks along the shores of large rivers, but today even gravel pits are being colonized. There can be little doubt that much of the increase is a result of decreasing persecution of this large and obvious bird that has always been seen as an enemy of the shell-fish industry.

Habitat: Shingle beaches and bars in large rivers, also gravel pits; outside the breeding season resorts to large estuaries as well as open shorelines and damp grass fields.

Locations: As a breeding bird oystercatchers breed right round the coasts of Britain save only where tourist development makes it impossible. They are thus absent from long stretches of the coast in the south and from much of the Yorkshire coast. Elsewhere they are abundant. Inland over most of Scotland and north-western England and some evidence of a continued spread inland to the heart of the country.

Winter Visitor: Large numbers (up to 200,000) winter in Britain, many gathering in really spectacular flocks at particularly favoured locations September is the peak month.

Locations: Burry 10,000; Dee 10,000; Dengie 5,000; Duddon 10,000; Exe 5,000; Foulness 5,000; Humber 2,500; Lindisfarne 2,500; Morecambe 25,000; Torridge-Taw 2,500; Ribble 5,000; Swale 5,000; The Wash 10,000; Solway 10,000; Eden 5,000; Inner Moray Firth 5,000; Cromarty Firth 2,500; Firth of Forth 5,000; Montrose Basin 2,500; Tay 2,500.

Avocet *Recurvirostra avosetta*

Resident: Avocets nest at a few East Anglian sites where they may form quite large colonies; they are, however, still rightly regarded as rare breeding birds. Since the re-colonization of 1947 only two major sites have been used with any degree of regularity – Havergate and Minsmere, both in Suffolk – though several peripheral colonies have been established and isolated pairs have bred at several spots along the east coast. As has been the case throughout its return, low rates of reproduction have prevented the species from really taking off and numbers still remain at less than 150 pairs. The work of the RSPB in safeguarding the two main sites has been crucial throughout.
Habitat: Shallow saline and freshwater lagoons with drying out islands and gently sloping banks.
Locations: Havergate and Minsmere; elsewhere decidedly rare.
Winter Visitor: A small flock regularly winters in the south-west.
Locations: Cargreen on the Tamar.

Stone-curlew *Burhinus oedicnemus*

Summer Visitor: This sole European representative of what is a remarkably widespread family of Old World birds is in grave danger of disappearing as a British breeding bird. Even over the last 20 years its numbers have seriously declined and now only 300–500 pairs breed here each year. It is confined to the south and east, and within that area to the chalklands and downs and to sundry heathlands. The major factor in the decline was undoubtedly the decimation of the rabbit population following myxamatosis outbreaks in the 1950s and the inevitable invasion of scrub that followed. Today stone-curlews nest mostly on arable land and are prone to harm from modern agricultural machinery. As a result most first clutches are lost. Usually arrives in mid-March and stays through to October, by which time it is gathered into small flocks.

Habitat: Open downs, sandy wastes, rabbit warrens, well-drained arable land.

Locations: Due to the rarity of the species and the ever-present danger from egg collectors exact locations cannot be given even where the birds nest in reserves: Wiltshire Downs; Marlborough Downs; Chilterns; Newmarket and adjacent heaths; Brecks; north Norfolk and east Suffolk coastal heaths; South Downs; Dungeness.

Little Ringed Plover *Charadrius dubius*

Summer Visitor: First breeding in Britain only as recently as 1938, the little ringed plover is now a well-established bird in England as far north as the Scottish border and west to the Welsh border country. This spread has been clearly linked to the huge increase in the use of concrete by the construction industry, the consequent demand for gravel and the creation of extraction pits. Strangely enough these pits are most suitable to the birds while they are in production, when lengthy shallow and bare margins are available – later they become overgrown and unsuitable. Today some 500 pairs breed regularly, arriving in late March and staying through to early October. Throughout Britain they are remarkably tolerant of disturbance and regularly lay replacement clutches for those lost to machinery.

Habitat: Gravel pit margins, but on the Continent mostly along the gravel margins of rivers.

Locations: There is barely a flooded gravel pit with bare open margins, or a reservoir under construction in England east of a line drawn from the Solent to the Dee, that is not a potential breeding site for little ringed plovers. Highest numbers are found in south-east England, north and south of London, and in the north Midlands. On passage appears at reservoirs and even coastal marshes.

Ringed Plover *Charadrius hiaticula*

Resident: In very few parts of the country can ringed plovers be really regarded as 'residents' and many certainly leave the country during the depths of winter, yet some always remain. About 5,000 pairs breed, mainly around our coasts, but many inland particularly in north-western England and Scotland. East Anglia has always had a strong though declining inland tradition in the Brecks and Fens. Peak numbers occur in the autumn when perhaps 20,000 may frequent our shores.

Habitat: Shingle and sandy beaches, farmland near the shore, shingle banks of rivers, reservoirs and large gravel pits.

Locations: Breeding on all coasts save for the over-touristy, and the extreme south-west and westermost Wales which must be regarded as being on the very edge of the species' range. Large autumn concent-rations: Blackwater 1,000; Calshot 500; Colne 500; Dee 2,500; Dengie 500; Duddon 500; Dyfi 1,000; Exe 500; Firth of Forth 500; Foulness 500; Guscar Rocks 500; Hamford 1,000; Langstone 500; Leigh 500; Medway 1,000; Morecambe 10,000; Moricambe 2,500; Ribble 1,000; Slimbridge 500; Solway 1,000; The Wash 1,000; Torridge-Taw 500.

Kentish Plover *Charadrius alexandrinus*

Passage Migrant: A former breeding bird that last nested in 1956 at Rye Harbour. Now only a rather scarce bird of passage to the south and east coasts of England. Elsewhere in the world the Kentish plover is one of the most widespread of all birds with a virtually cosmopolitan distribution. Over most of its range it is essentially a coastal bird, but in eastern Africa, central Asia and estern North America it is well established inland.

Habitat: Sandy and shingle beaches and margins, salt pans and other waters, deltas, etc.

Locations: Though any spot on the south and east coasts may produce a Kentish plover, particularly in May or August-September, the marshes of East Anglia are by far the most regularly used; Minsmere, Cley.

Dotterel *Charadrius morinellus*

Summer Visitor: Up to a hundred pairs of dotterel breed each year on the highest mountains they can find in Britain, but also increasingly on

Top A regular autumn migrant in highly variable numbers, the **curlew sandpiper** breeds in arctic Siberia and may be sought among flocks of **dunlin** in August and September.
Bottom A **wryneck** at its nest box. A rare summer visitor that has declined to the point of extinction in southern England, but which has started to colonise Scotland in recent years. Best sought on the east coast in autumn.

Top A scarce breeder in historical times, the **spoonbill** is now a rare passage migrant that is regular only on the marshes of East Anglia. It breeds as near as Holland and may one day do so at Minsmere.

Bottom Part of a huge flock of **pink-footed geese** in Kinross-shire in Scotland. Such spectacular flights may be seen in several parts of that country.

large and bare plateaux. Today, though not as numerous as before, the species is as widespread as it has ever been. Only a few years ago it was more or less confined to the high tops of the Cairngorm–Grampian chain. Now it can be found north to Sutherland, in the border country, and in northern England and North Wales. While it has spread elsewhere its main strongholds have been increasingly invaded by hikers and skiers. Most birds arrive at the end of April and stay through to September.

Habitat: Bare open mountain tops away from snow drifts, also on tundra and in Holland on polders below sea level; on passage also on dry wastes which are frequently traditional stop-overs.

Locations: Spotting a dotterel is never easy. Suitably equipped, the birder must walk the high tops keeping an eye for an extremely effectively camouflaged bird quietly walking away. Visit Cairngorms via ski-lift; Grampians; Monadliath.

Golden Plover *Pluvialis apricaria*

Resident: Resplendent in their black and gold plumage of summer, golden plovers can be found in all the upland regions of Britain, though it is in the Penines and in the Highlands of Scotland that they become common. Some 30,000 pairs breed in the country as a whole, but almost half of that number are found in the Highlands. In the drabber garb of winter thes birds form good sized flocks and then wander nomadically over the countryside often joining flocks of lapwings in the fields, but also resorting to marshes and estuaries. Their distinctive call 'tlui' is uttered in flight and can often be heard as they migrate overhead at night, even in large cities.

Habitat: Grass moorland in summer; in winter they resort to flooded grassland, grazing, arable fields, marshes and estuaries.

Locations: Dartmoor 10 pairs; Wales 600 pairs; Pennines and Yorkshire Moors 7,500; Border 3,800; Highlands 15,000; Islands 2,000.

Winter Visitor: Large influx of Icelandic and Continental birds which can be distinguished from our own breeding birds in spring by their much more extensive black underparts. Winter population widespread, but with some very large concentrations at particularly favoured spots; total about 200,000.

Locations: Burry; Blackwater; Chichester; Cley and Blakeney; Colne;

Crouch; Exe; Firth of Forth; Foulness; Hamford Water; Hayle; Kingsbridge; Lindisfarne; Morecambe; Moricambe; Ouse Washes; Ribble; Slimbridge; Solway; Swale; Tamar; Torridge-Taw; The Wash. Though these locations have strong regular populations there are many other estuaries and wetlands which support good numbers of golden plovers, but which are often ignored by wader enthusiasts. The birds are also present in many other habitats and are widespread throughout the country.

Grey Plover *Pluvialis squatarola*

Winter Visitor: A high arctic breeding bird with a circumpolar distribution across the tundra zones of Siberia, Alaska and Canada. Absent from Greenland to Scandinavia. Passage extends from March to June and again from July through to October, and large numbers of birds pass along our coasts to and from winter quarters further south in Europe and the Atlantic coast of North Africa. Some 12,000 birds winter in Britain and are confined to estuaries and open shores. Inland this is a decidedly rare bird.

Habitat: Tundra; on passage and in winter along muddy shores and estuaries. Often ignores one estuary to concentrate on another.

Locations: Blackwater 1,000; Burry 500; Calshott 250; Chichester 1,000; Colne 250; Dee 500; Dengie 1,000; Exe 500; Eden 250; Firth of Forth 250; Foulness 250; Hamford Water 1,000; Keyhaven 250; Langstone 500; Leigh 500; Lindisfarne 250; Morecambe 250; Moricambe 250; Medway 1,000; Pagham 250; Ribble 1,000; Solway 500; Stour 500; Swale 1,000; Thames 250; The Wash 5,000.

Lapwing *Vanellus vanellus*

Resident: One of the most familiar and successful of British birds, this attractive wader breeds right across the Palearctic. Several hundred thousand individuals breed and these numbers are joined by immigrants to form the winter population. Their success stems entirely from the extraordinary range of habitats that they are able to occupy successfully both while breeding and in winter. Though prone to hard weather that can effectively freeze over their feeding grounds, they are flexible enough to move out quickly and make journeys of even several hundreds of miles to find open ground. Their only other serious threat, the collection of 'plovers' eggs' for the restaurant market, was eliminated earlier this century.

Habitat: Extremely varied; arable, grassland, moorland, marshes; in winter on estuaries, floods, grass, arable and marshland.

Locations: Absent as a breeding bird only from a few of the highest Scottish hills, and parts of the extreme south-west and south-west Wales. In winter becomes rather scarce in Scotland, but abundant in southern England. Large concentrations at many places, though few larger than at the Ouse Washes.

Knot *Calidris canutus*

Winter Visitor: Despite breeding only in the highest of high arctic regions from the Canadian islands, through Greenland, Spitzbergen and northernmost Siberia, the knot is one of the most numerous birds on British winter estuaries. It is, however, also remarkably concentrated with huge numbers favoring a few localities while apparently very similar wetlands nearby are totally ignored. Knot arrive on our shores from late July to November with some birds moving through to winter further south along the Atlantic coasts of Europe and West Africa. Some 300,000 spend the winter with us until returning northwards from March to May. Ringing has shown that our birds are drawn from both west and east.

Habitat: Arctic tundra; muddy estuaries and open shores.

Locations: About 50,000 are found on the Ribble, on Morecambe Bay and on The Wash; Burry 10,000; Cromarty 2,500; Dee 25,000; Dengie 5,000; Duddon 2,500; Eden 2,500; Firth of Forth 10,000; Foulness 10,000; Humber 10,000; Lindisfarne 10,000; Moricambe 25,000; Solway 10,000; Swale 5,000; Teesmouth 10,000. Other flocks of over 1,000 individuals are comparatively rare.

Sanderling *Calidris alba*

Winter Visitor: Breeding as far north as ice-free land exists, sanderlings flock southwards to reach our shores from mid-July and stay on to winter through to May. Though brown and white in their summer haunts, by the time they reach us they are the lightest grey birds along the shoreline. In small trips they scurry backwards and forwards moving up and down with each successive wave, sometimes courting disaster but never quite getting caught. This behaviour alone makes them easily identifiable. Though some 10,000 winter, there are better numbers during spring and autumn passage when at least twice as many may be present. However, they are widespread rather than concentrated.

Habitat: Arctic tundra; sandy and rocky shores; seldom found on muddy estuaries and even rarer inland.

Locations: Most common in north and west with really good numbers along the shellsand beaches of the Hebrides in May and at three major estuaries; Chichester 500; Dee 10,000; Morecambe 10,000; Moricambe 500; Ribble 10,000; Teesmouth 500; The Wash 2,500.

Little Stint *Calidris minuta*

Passage Migrant: Little stints breed eastwards from northern Scandinavia across northermost Siberia, but do not reach either the Bering Straits or North America. They are summer visitors to these hostile regions and migrate southwards to winter in tropical Africa and Asia where they are often very numerous. On both passages Britain lies westward of the main route, though in autumn good (though variable) numbers can occur. It is thus regular though never in the large flocks found further south and east.

Habitat: Arctic tundra; outside breeding season frequents marshes, salt pans and estuaries.

Locations: Being a southern and eastern migrant through Europe the nearer to those areas within Britain the better the chances of seeing little stints. Spring passage is very thin. In autumn juveniles arrive by early August and the species is present throughout September at good marshes such as Holme, Cley, Walberswick, Minsmere, Sheppey, north Kent, Rye Harbour, Pagham, Farlington and Poole. Elsewhere it is decidedly scarce. Small numbers winter in the south-west, e.g. at Dawlish.

Temminck's Stint *Calidris temminckii*

Summer Visitor: A few pairs of this tiny but tame wader nest annually among the Highland hills and bogs of Scotland. They are well established in one location, but are undoubtedly present in many more areas than are ever published. Though they are well worth looking for anywhere in the Highland region in late May and June their locations are not likely to be made public in the forseeable future.

Habitat: Upland bogs and marshes with or without willow scrub. Outside breeding season frequents freshwater margins both inland and near the coast.

Locations: Highlands of Scotland.

Passage Migrant: A scattering of Temminck's stints passes through Britain in May and June and again in August and September.

Locations: They are never numerous and are as likely to occur at an inland reservoir as at one of the south and east coast bird resorts.

Pectoral Sandpiper *Calidris melanotos*

Passage Migrant: This is the most regular of all North American birds this side of the Atlantic and seems to be either increasing or becoming ever more familiar to British bird-watchers. In Ireland the species even occurs in small flocks, though singles are the rule in Britain. Its characteristic call 'chirrup' draws attention to it even in mixed flocks of shorebirds.

Habitat: Variable from freshwater margins to salt pans and estuaries.

Locations: Concentrated in south and west in autumn with main passage in September and early October, though there are regular records in July and August; Isles of Scilly, Marazion, Hayle, Farlington, Cley, Gibraltar Point are the regular haunts worth checking, though anywhere along the south coast can produce birds.

Curlew Sandpiper *Calidris ferruginea*

Passage Migrant: Breeds only in remotest central northern Siberia and

migrates southward to winter in Africa, Asia and as far as New
Zealand and Australia. Unfortunately Britain is west of their normal
route so that each autumn only a few pass along our shores.
Occasionally, however, quite large numbers do occur. Superficially
similar to the dunlin, but taller, more elegant, with longer decurved bill
and diagnostic white rump.

Habitat: Arctic tundra: outside breeding season frequents marshes and
estuaries, as well as freshwater margins.

Locations: The south and east do best with Cley, Minsmere, Sheppey,
north Kent, Sandwich Bay, Rye Harbour, Pagham, Farlington which
all have birds most years. August and September are best months;
spring migrants are decidedly scarce.

Purple Sandpiper *Calidris maritima*

Summer Visitor: First bred in 1978 when a pair hatched three young in
Scotland.

Winter Visitor: A totally marine sandpiper that is decidedly rare inland
outside the breeding season. Its particular habitat, rocky shores with
strong growths of seaweed, make it easy to locate, though its effective
camouflage often makes it difficult to find. It enjoys a circumpolar
breeding distribution that includes Iceland and Scandinavia and
winters as far north as there are ice-free shorelines.

Habitat: Arctic tundra: outside breeding season is confined to rocky
shorelines often in company with turnstones.

Locations: In Britain rocky shorelines are found mostly in the north and
west and it is here that purple sandpipers should be sought. From
Devon and Cornwall to Scotland they are common with a winter
population of 10,000 to 20,000 in total. Elsewhere, though scarce, they
are regular in small numbers on breakwaters, piers, and odd rocky
outcrops.

Passage Migrant: Numbers do pass through on their way further south
from late July and again in spring to late May.

Locations: As in winter.

Dunlin *Calidris alpina*

Resident: Different populations of dunlins are present in Britain throughout the year, for it breeds here and is both a passage migrant and a winter visitor to our shores. As a breeding bird it is confined to the hilly districts of the north and west, whereas outside the breeding season it flocks along our shores, often in incredible numbers. It is by far the most common shorebird in Britain and some flocks number over 50,000 individuals. It is also found inland, though in smaller numbers, and never in large flocks.

Habitat: Moors and bogs, freshwater margins, sewage works, estuaries, open shorelines, rocky shores, and so on. Remarkably catholic.

Locations: This 'standard' British shorebird is numerous and widespread and may turn up in any aquatic habitat on passage, particularly in autumn. Large winter concentrations at: Blackwater 10,000; Breydon 5,000; Burry 10,000; Calshot 5,000; Chichester 20,000; Chittening Worth 5,000; Colne 5,000; Dee 25,000; Dengie 5,000; Duddon 10,000; Eden 5,000; Exe 10,000; Firth of Forth 10,000; Foulness 10,000; Hamford 10,000; Humber 10,000; Keyhaven 5,000; Langstone 10,000; Leigh 10,000; Lindisfarne 10,000; Medway 10,000; Inner Moray Firth 5,000; Morecambe 25,000; Moricambe 10,000; Pagham 5,000; Ribble 25,000; Solway 10,000; Stour 10,000; Swale 5,000; Tamar 5,000; Tay 5,000; Teesmouth 10,000; Thames 5,000; The Wash 25,000; Torridge-Taw 5,000. This list also effectively summarizes the most important estuaries in Britain for waders.

Ruff *Philomachus pugnax*

Resident: Small numbers of ruff have re-established themselves in Britain after becoming more or less extinct as a breeding bird soon after the turn of the century. In 1963 the species was found breeding on the Ouse Washes and over a hundred males (ruff) gather to lek (display) to their mates (reeves) within the safety of the string of nature reserves that are now established to protect this important site. Elsewhere breeding is at best sporadic, though north Norfolk has a regular spring lek.

Habitat: Grassland that has been flooded in winter; also marshy margins and tundra.

Locations: Cley has a lek; Ouse Washes have various reserves – try RSPB.

Passage Migrant: Large numbers of ruff pass through the south and east of the country in both spring and autumn. They are particularly numerous in the latter season for spring tends to take them further east through Europe. Small numbers increasingly stay on to winter.

Locations: All the usual south and east coast marshes have ruff in August and September and there are usually good numbers inland as well. Large reservoirs such as Rutland Water and Grafham, as well as sewage works are favoured.

Jack Snipe *Lymnocryptes minimus*

Winter Visitor: The jack snipe, which is a smaller version of the common snipe but with a shorter bill and less zig-zagging flight, breeds from northern Scandinavia eastwards across northern Eurasia. It is a winter visitor to Britain and is probably most numerous in autumn, when birds bound for the western part of the Continent pass through. It is most frequently found in association with common snipe and is located by watching for bill and behaviour when flushed.

Habitat: Marshes and bogs; found in all freshwater habitats that support a good growth of emergent vegetation.

Locations: Absent only from extreme west and north of country. All areas with snipe are potential jack snipe locations.

Snipe *Gallinago gallinago*

Resident: A very widespread breeding bird that is also an abundant winter visitor. Snipe are cryptically coloured and can easily be overlooked among the dense growth of vegetation they favour. Once flushed, however, their long bills and erratic towering flight are quite unmistakable. In spring they have a special 'drumming' display flight in which the stiffened outer tail feathers are 'bleated' through the air to produce a vibrant sound. Approaching 100,000 pairs breed in Britain occupying virtually every corner of the country, though there are considerable areas of the south-west where the birds are absent.

Habitat: Marshes, floods, lakesides, ditches and other areas with mud and good ground cover.

Locations: Can be looked for in any suitable habitat throughout the country; Tiree and the Outer Hebrides have the reputation of being the best snipe-shooting sites in Europe, so they must have good winter populations.

Woodcock *Scolopax rusticola*

Resident: A widespread and numerous breeding bird whose numbers are augmented by a considerable winter immigration. Never gregarious and always crepuscular, woodcock are never easy to see at any time of the year. They inhabit mostly deciduous woodland and the best chance of seeing one is during the spring and summer 'roding' season. At this time the birds circle high above their territories uttering a distinctive 'tissuk' note. They may then pass over the same spot again and again at a few minutes' interval. At other times of the year they may be flushed, but dusk is always the best time to look for them.
Habitat: Damp and marshy spots in deciduous woodland and among new conifer plantations.
Locations: Absent from the Fens, from most of the south-west, from south-west Wales, and from the Outer Hebrides, Orkneys and Shetlands. Otherwise may be sought throughout the country.

Black-tailed Godwit *Limosa limosa*

Resident: A few pairs of this large and elegant wader have nested every year since 1952, after an absence of a century. Gradually numbers have built up to reach a present peak of about sixty pairs, the vast majority of which a e found on the Ouse Washes. Larger numbers occur on passage particularly in mid-May in East Anglia. However, wintering numbers have also increased to well over 4,000 individuals, though much larger numbers are present in autumn.
Habitat: Flooded grassland; outside breeding season on marshes and estuaries.
Locations: Breeds on Ouse Washes (over 80% of total); on Norfolk and Suffolk coasts; in northern Kent; in Somerset; and a different population in Shetland, Orkney and Caithness. Passage through most estuaries, particularly in south and east where winter flocks occur: Bridgwater 1,000; Burry 250; Chichester 1,000; Dee 1,000; Eden 250;

Exe 1,000; Hamford 250; Langstone 500; Medway 500; Moricambe 250; Newtown 250; Pagham 250; Poole 500; Ribble 1,000; Stour 1,000; Swale 500; Tamar 500.

Bar-tailed Godwit *Limosa lapponica*

Winter Visitor: Breeding across northern Siberia, large numbers of bar-tailed godwits come southwards to winter in Europe, over half of them in Britain. They are essentially estuarine birds that spend most of their time probing deeply in inter-tidal mud for invertebrates and, with their long straight bills, can be confused only with their more elegant relative the black-tailed godwit. Unlike that species the bar-tailed godwit lacks a prominent white wing-bar.

Habitat: Marshes and tundra pools; in winter estuaries and shorelines with mud banks.

Locations: About 40,000 bar-tailed godwits winter in Britain, mostly in the north-west and east on the larger estuaries: Burry 500; Chichester 1,000; Cromarty Firth 1,000; Dee 5,000; Dengie 500; Eden 2,500; Exe 1,000; Firth of Forth 2,500; Foulness 2,500; Inner Moray Firth 2,500; Lindisfarne 5,000; Morecambe 10,000; Moricambe 5,000; Ribble 10,000; Solway 2,500; Swale 1,000; Tay 1,000; Teesmouth 500; The Wash 5,000.

Whimbrel *Numenius phaeopus*

Summer Visitor: Although it breeds right round the northern hemisphere in the boreal zone, the whimbrel finds itself at the southern edge of its range in Britain. By the 1930s it was more or less confined to Shetland and was down to 50 or so pairs. The climatic changes that have so affected the bird population of Britain over the past 30 years or so have also contributed to an increase and spread of the whimbrel. Today some 200 pairs can be found in various parts of the Highlands and Islands, though a third of that number inhabits the island of Unst in Shetland.

Habitat: Moorland with bogs, marshes, heather; outside breeding season found on marshes, estuaries and open shores.

Locations: Unst, Yell, Fetlar and mainland in Shetland; Orkney, Caithness, Sutherland and the northern, more acidic, parts of the Outer Hebrides. Without a doubt Unst is the island to look over, but beware of undue disturbance.

Passage Migrant: Good numbers of whimbrel pass through on both spring and autumn passages. Spring passage is usually more pronounced in the west and also less prolonged with smaller parties of birds. Autumn passage is more leisurely and widespread with birds on all coasts and occasionally inland. An unusual gathering has developed in the south-west in recent years.

Locations: All coastal marshes and estuaries in autumn with a massive total of 1,000 birds in Bridgwater Bay. In spring Isles of Scilly, western beaches and particularly Outer Hebrides get strongest passage.

Curlew *Numenius arquata*

Resident: An Old World wader that finds its westernmost breeding haunts in Britain where it is both widespread and abundant. Only disturbance prevents the curlew from occupying large areas of lowland Britain, while its catholic choice of habitat enables it to exploit virtually every moorland worthy of the name. Only in the Outer Hebrides and Wester Ross is it thin on the ground, while in parts of the Pennines and Wales it is fairly abundant.

Habitat: Grass and heather moors, heathland, marshes; outside breeding season frequents estuaries, marshes and open shorelines as well as grasslands and arable fields.

Locations: Breeds in almost every corner of Britain north of a line from the Severn to Flamborough Head. South of that line it breeds on moors such as Dartmoor, the Dorset Heaths, the Brecks and at many places on the chalk. Total population is about 50,000 pairs.

Winter Visitor: The British population of curlews is increased considerably by an influx from the Continent. At such times, that is from October to March, these birds are found on all coasts and in large numbers on many estuaries.

Locations: Burry 2,500; Camel 1,000; Colne 2,500; Cromarty Firth 1,000; Dee 5,000; Dengie 2,500; Duddon 1,000; Exe 1,000; Firth of Forth 2,500; Foulness 5,000; Guscar Rocks 1,000; Humber 2,500; Hamford 2,500; Leigh 1,000; Lindisfarne 1,000; Medway 2,500; Montrose Basin

1,000; Morecambe 25,000; Moricambe 10,000; North Kent 1,000; Ribble 1,000; Solway 5,000; Stour 1,000; Swale 1,000; Tamar 1,000; The Wash 10,000; Torridge-Taw 2,500.

Spotted Redshank *Tringa erythropus*

Passage Migrant: Breeding in the tundra zone from northern Scandinavia across Siberia almost to the Pacific and wintering from Africa across Asia to India and beyond, the spotted redshank is a passage migrant to Britain with a well-established, though small, wintering population in the south-west. In its all-black breeding plumage this is one of the most distinctive and beautiful of all shorebirds, and some birds can be seen in this garb even as far south as East Anglia in late spring (June) and early autumn (July). However, though it is similar to the redshank in winter plumage it is always greyer and has longer bill and legs that give it a more elegant appearance.

Habitat: Edge of the taiga zone with heather moors and scattered trees; outside breeding season frequents marshes and floods frequently some distance inland.

Locations: Mostly the south and west coasts, but with regular numbers at Cley, Minsmere, etc. Along the south coast there are small winter flocks at Medway, The Gins, Exe, Tamar.

Redshank *Tringa totanus*

Resident: Some 30,000 pairs of redshanks breed in Britain, and although many of these move southwards and westwards to winter, their places are taken by immigrants from abroad, particularly from Iceland. As a result the total population remains steady at about 80,000 birds. This is a very successful species in Britain occupying a variety of different habitats from coastal marshes and wet meadows to high moorland bogs. Its familiar 'tulip' call is as much a part of the estuarine scene as the call of the curlew, while its summer alarm is as annoying in its effect on the other birds as any other marshland 'watchdog'. Its long red legs preclude confusion with any other British bird save the spotted redshank and occasional over-bright ruff.

Habitat: Marshes, damp meadows, moorland with boggy patches and lakes/pools; outside breeding season frequents estuaries, marshes and open rocky shorelines.

Locations: Breeds over upland Britain, but absent from Dartmoor and from much of Wales. In lowland England it is widespread but nowhere numerous. In winter there are large concentrations at Ouse Washes; Beauly Firth 1,000; Blackwater 5,000; Bridgwater 1,000; Burry 2,500; Calshot 2,500; Chichester 2,500; Colne 2,500; Cromarty Firth 2,500; Crouch 1,000; Dengie 1,000; Duddon 2,500; Eden 2,500; Exe 1,000; Firth of Forth 5,000; Foulness 5,000; Hamford Water 2,500; Humber 2,500; Inner Moray Firth 2,500; Keyhaven 1,000; Langstone 2,500; Leigh 2,500; Lindisfarne 2,500; Medway 2,500; Montrose Basin 2,500; Moricambe 5,000; Poole 1,000; Ribble 5,000; Solway 5,000; Stour 5,000; Swale 1,000; Tay 2,500; Tamar 2,500; Teesmouth 1,000; Thames 1,000; The Wash 10,000; Torridge-Taw 1,000; Ythan 1,000.

Greenshank *Tringa nebularia*

Summer Visitor: Greenshanks find in Britain one of their southernmost outposts in a distribution that extends right across Siberia to the Pacific. Some 500–750 pairs breed each year in the Highlands and Islands, but there is also a passage of Continental birds that is particularly apparent on the east and south coasts in autumn, and a small wintering population in the south-west. Unlike so many waders, greenshanks regularly appear at many inland waters and feed as happily around freshwater margins as they do on coastal creeks. They are usually encountered singly or in small groups and never form really large flocks. As a result their numbers are very difficult to estimate.

Habitat: Moorland usually with a scattering of trees or dwarf vegetation; outside breeding season at freshwater margins, creeks and backwaters, estuaries, but seldom on open shore.

Locations: Most frequent on autumn passage from July through to October both inland and along the coast. No notable concentrations. Spring passage extends through April and May.

Green Sandpiper *Tringa ochropus*

Passage Migrant: There are two proven records of green sandpipers breeding in Britain, in Westmorland in 1917 and Inverness in 1959, but numbers regularly pass through southern and eastern England on both passages. In autumn the birds are more numerous and in less of a hurry and can then be seen, usually singly, on marshes and along dykes and floods. Most have passed through by November, though small numbers stay on for the winter when they frequent even quite small streams.

Habitat: Marshes, floods, stream margins; never on open shore.

Locations: None specific, but best looked for in autumn in south and east of country both inland and along the coastal marshes.

Wood Sandpiper *Tringa glareola*

Summer Visitor: Though they occasionally bred during the last century, it was not until 1959 that wood sandpipers really became established as British breeding birds. In that year a pair bred in Sutherland and, although numbers have varied immensely, they have returned every year since. Outside the breeding season good numbers pass through on passage, particularly in the south and east, but these are as nothing compared with the huge concentrations that occur in the Camargue in France and further east. Britain must thus be regarded as being on the very edge of the species' range in every respect.

Habitat: Marshy woodlands with lochs and lakes; outside the breeding season occurs mostly on freshwater marshes, often considerable distances inland.

Locations: Breeds in Sutherland and Caithness, and in Inverness north and south of the Great Glen. South and east coast marshes, margins of large reservoirs and lake margins are used on passage.

Common Sandpiper *Actitis hypoleucos*

Summer Visitor: A thinly-spread species that may appear to be more abundant than it actually is by virtue of being solitary and occurring in a wide variety of different habitats. The total breeding population is probably less than 40,000 pairs, though doubtless numbers are increased by passage migrants in both spring and autumn. The species' habit of continually bobbing makes it readily identifiable and its propensity to occur at virtually any area of fresh water from a mountain stream to a village pond makes it one of our more familiar waders.

Habitat: Freshwater margins, breeding mostly along hilly streams, but occurs outside the breeding season on marshes, floods, lakesides and ponds. Seldom on seashores.

Locations: Breeds along most rivers and streams north of a line drawn from the Severn to Teesmouth. Numerous in Wales, the Pennines and Lake District, the Borders and Scottish hills and the Highlands and Islands. Thin on the ground in Shetland and Orkney, it is nevertheless numerous in the Outer Hebrides. In lowland England it is thinly spread over fast-running streams, though it is absent from the apparently suitable waters of Dartmoor.

Passage Migrant: Passes through the whole of Britain in spring and autumn, when it occurs at reservoirs, ponds, etc.

Locations: None specific.

Turnstone *Arenaria interpres*

Winter Visitor: Throughout the year turnstones are totally coastal birds. They breed from the coasts of Scandinavia right across the arctic coastline of Siberia as far as the Pacific and onwards along the coasts of Alaska and Canada, where they are known as the 'ruddy turnstone'. In winter they move southwards to the coasts of Britain where they frequent rocky shorelines, along with purple sandpipers, as much as they frequent estuaries. Though they will also exploit coastal marshes, they are very rarely seen inland. They are generally gregarious, forming small flocks 20–40 strong, but never occur in the huge packs favoured by several other shorebirds.

Habitat: Coastal islets; outside breeding season found on all shore-lines, but particularly rocky ones.

Locations: About 10,000 turnstones winter on our shores with a definite bias to the north and west: Burry 1,000; Calshot 500; Camel 250; Chichester 250; Chittening Worth 250; Colne 250; Dee 500; Dengie 1,000; Duddon 250; Exe 500; Firth of Forth 1,000; Foulness 250; Hamford Water 250; Humber 500; Inner Moray Firth 250; Leigh 500; Lindisfarne 250; Morecambe 2,500; Moricambe 500; Montrose Basin

250; Ribble 500; Solway 500; Stour 250; Swale 500; Tamar 250; Teesmouth 250; The Wash 1,000; Torridge-Taw 250.

Red-necked Phalarope *Phalaropus lobatus*

Summer Visitor: Some 30 to 40 pairs of red-necked phalaropes breed in Scotland every year and there is some indication of a gradual decline in numbers. Despite the full protection of the law there is no doubt that these attractive and confiding little birds are still persecuted by egg collectors, an activity made all the easier by the tenacity with which the birds cling to their traditional breeding sites. Outside the breeding season these phalaropes spend the winter at sea and occur on passage along coasts but inland only when storm-driven. However, October gales usually bring a few (sometimes a huge wreck) to our shores.
Habitat: Small marshy pools; outside breeding season at sea, inland only storm-driven.
Locations: Breeding is confined to Shetland, particularly Fetlar; Outer Hebrides, Balranald, etc; and Tiree. They do not arrive until the later half of May. Storm-driven birds mostly occur in the west in October, but also inland and on the east coast.

Grey Phalarope *Phalaropus fulicarius*

Passage Migrant: Grey phalaropes breed right across the Northern Hemisphere, though no nearer to Britain than south-western Iceland where there is only a small population. The rest of their year is spent at sea and, at the end of the breeding season, they migrate through the Atlantic and may then be driven inshore by the gales of October and November. At this time they are more or less annual in south-west England, and may occur in huge flocks 1,000 or more strong. The comparative lack of birds in western Scotland indicates a trans-Atlantic origin for these birds. They may, on occasion, be blown inland and to the south and east coasts.
Habitat: Tundra marshes and shorelines; outside breeding season at sea; onshore only storm-driven.
Locations: Isles of Scilly, St. Ives Island, and other south-western headlands and bird resorts.

Pomarine Skua *Stercorarius pomarinus*

Passage Migrant: This tundra breeding species enjoys a virtually circumpolar breeding distribution, wintering southwards in the world's oceans as far as New Zealand and Peru. Numbers pass from Siberia through the Denmark Strait and between Shetland and Iceland to gain the open Atlantic where they move southwards to south-west Africa. At this time they may be seen off western coasts and some even straggle into the North Sea and Channel. The spring movement is briefer and more concentrated with occasional flocks, rather than individuals, passing off prominent headlands.

Habitat: Tundra with marshy pools; at other times at sea, frequently out of sight of land.

Locations: Though pomarine skuas appear on most coasts from time to time, Spurn and Cley are regularly favoured in autumn. In spring, passage is heaviest during the first half of May when good numbers may be seen off west coast headlands. Up-Channel movements are often detectable at Dungeness.

Arctic Skua *Stercorarius parasiticus*

Summer Visitor: Though it is not as numerous as the great skua as a breeding bird, it is far more widespread and generally rather easier to see than its larger cousin. By 1970 just over a thousand pairs bred in Britain, but within four years one large colony had jumped from 230 to over 600 pairs, indicating that a veritable population explosion had taken place. The species now breeds from Shetland through Orkney to the Outer Hebrides and southwards to Jura.

Habitat: Heather and grass moors with bogs, usually near the coast, but also some distances inland. Outside the breeding season migrates southwards to occupy the rich oceans of the Southern Hemisphere. Parasitic hunting habits.

Locations: Over half of British population breed in Shetland where they occur on all major islands – with large numbers of Fetlar and Fair Isle. Numerous and expanding rapidly in Orkney. Southern and coastal Caithness has a growing population and there are isolated pairs or colonies at Handa, the Summer Isles, Coll, Oronsay and Jura. In the

Outer Hebrides it is numerous on North Uist and northern and eastern Lewis.

Passage Migrant: Regular migrant along all coasts presumably including large numbers of continental (Scandinavian) birds. Concentrations occur at some estuaries where large populations of terns are themselves attracted by masses of sand-eels.

Locations: All coasts, but Northumberland at Teesmouth and other areas nearby boast large concentrations in late summer and autumn.

Long-tailed Skua *Stercorarius longicaudus*

Passage Migrant: Long-tailed skuas enjoy a circumpolar breeding distribution in the northernmost ice-free areas of the world. Their population and breeding success is totally linked to that of small arctic rodents, particularly lemmings, and in years when such animals are scarce or absent they do not even bother to attempt breeding. Outside the breeding season they are largely pelagic and on passage pass well north of the British Isles out into the open Atlantic. They are thus scarce on our shores.

Habitat: Arctic tundra; outside breeding season at sea.

Locations: Regularly identified only off coasts of Northumberland and Norfolk, but doubtless appears elsewhere unrecorded.

Great Skua *Stercorarius skua*

Summer Visitor: A total of almost 4,000 pairs of great skuas, or 'bonxies' as they are called in Shetland, breed in Scotland. In 1890 there were probably not more than 100 pairs and the recovery of the species owes much to the private pioneer conservationists, the Edmonstons of Buness, who owned Hermaness in northern Unst. Today these birds are widespread throughout Shetland and have spread to Orkney, to Caithness and Sutherland, to North Rona and Lewis, and to St. Kilda. The increase and spread has returned the great skua to many of its old haunts, but over two-thirds of the total is confined to the isle of Foula.

Habitat: Open grass and heather-covered moors and bogs near the sea and adjacent to large seabird colonies. At other seasons may be found at sea, piratically cruising the oceans.

Locations: Though great skuas nest on the Scottish mainland there are comparatively few easily accessible spots to see them. John o' Groats is easily found and the seabird cliffs to the east and south are regularly harried; similarly Dunnet Head, the most northerly point of the British mainland. Fair Isle is reliable, but there is no great population, though it is easier to visit than Foula where huge numbers are to be found. Hermaness and Fetlar are still the easiest places to see large numbers of great skuas. Try the Loch of Cliff at the head of Burra Firth on Unst.

Passage Migrant: Only scattered records around the British coasts, though storm-driven migrants can be noted off southern and western England.

Locations: Western hot spots such as Hilbre and St Ives Island, as well as large inlets on all coasts where the feeding is easy.

Mediterranean Gull *Larus melanocephalus*

Summer Visitor: A rare summer visitor in very small numbers that has bred on a handful of occasions in Hampshire. Unfortunately most records concern hybrids and hybrid pairs crossed with, or mated to, black-headed gulls in a huge gullery. Common particularly in eastern Mediterranean.

Habitat: Sea coasts, marshes, harbours, sometimes inland among other gulls.

Locations: Needs Oar Point Nature Reserve in Hampshire is the only known breeding site. However, the large number of black-headed gulls makes a sighting very unlikely. Access restricted.

Passage Migrant and Winter Visitor: Regular in Britain in small numbers every autumn and winter; certainly scarce in spring.

Locations: Mostly confined to south and east coasts and there are several instances of birds returning to winter in the same location year after year, e.g. Hartlepool, Covehithe. May be seen almost anywhere between eastern Scotland and Cornwall.

Little Gull *Larus minutus*

Summer Visitor: An extremely rare breeding bird with the occasional pair laying eggs and conceivably rearing young. It breeds at several spots from the shores of the North Sea southwards and eastwards through Europe into Asia. It is a tiny, tern-like gull that is quite unlike any other British species.

Habitat: Frequents marshes in summer and for preference at other times. Also found on passage along shores, at lakes and reservoirs often some distance inland.

Locations: The Fen district especially the Ouse Washes and the southern shores of The Wash are the known breeding haunts.

Passage Migrant: Though it can be seen at many spots along the south and east coasts the little gull often forms quite large flocks that stay off-passage at several well-established localities.

Locations: Kilconquhar Loch and nearby Elie Ness, Buddon Burn and Hurworth Burn are good spots in Scotland and the north-east while Radipole is reliable in the south. Large lowland reservoirs in London and Midlands are regular inland haunts.

Sabine's Gull *Larus sabini*

Passage Migrant: A Nearctic breeder that crosses the Atlantic to winter off the coasts of tropical West Africa, it passes through the Bay of Biscay and along the coasts of Spain and Portugal in some numbers every autumn. Southerly and westerly winds regularly drift numbers of birds to the south-western approaches and occasionally up-Channel.

Habitat: Breeds on tundra, spends rest of year at sea generally out of sight of land.

Locations: Cornwall has the bulk of records of this North American gull and St Ives Island the majority of these as storm-blown birds in September and October make their way out of the Bristol Channel. The crossing from Penzance to the Isles of Scilly is a good spot at such times. South coast headlands are much less reliable.

Black-headed gull *Larus ridibundus*

Resident: Some 150,000 to 250,000 pairs of black-headed gulls breed in Britain and the bird is widespread inland and along the coast. Nevertheless, there are some remarkable colonies including one of

20,000 pairs at Needs Oar Point, and 10,000 pairs at the famous Ravenglass gullery. With the single possible exception of the south-west there can hardly be a spot in the country from which it is not possible to see black-headed gulls within a few miles, virtually every day of the year.

Habitat: Coasts, estuaries, inland reservoirs, rubbish dumps, parks and playing fields, city centres, lakes, arable land; indeed virtually any-where that this adaptable bird can glean a living alongside man.

Locations: Needs Oar Point, Ravenglass, Tentsmuir Point (with 8,000), Lincolnshire Wash, Scolt Head and Blakeney, Essex coast and Dungeness all have good colonies as do the Pennines, the Welsh hills and the whole of upland Scotland.

Passage Migrant and Winter Visitor: Huge numbers of continental birds move westwards in winter to pass through Britain or to stay on to winter. The majority come from Scandinavia and northern Europe, but some come from eastern France and from as far as Czechoslovakia. In winter they are widespread and abundant throughout Britain.

Locations: All coasts, save the extreme north and south-west, and most inland areas within range of a safe roost.

Common Gull *Larus canus*

Resident: The common gull belies its name by being decidedly uncommon as a breeding bird throughout most of Britain. With a couple of notable exceptions it is confined to Scotland, where it forms mainly small colonies both inland and along the coast. While a distribution map shows it to be widespread it is by no means numerous, being quite thinly spread on the ground. An apparent cluster of sites in Anglesey is in fact no more than a few isolated pairs nesting in large herring gull colonies. The total British population may be of the order of 40,000 pairs.

Habitat: Moorland, marshes and bogs with movements to coasts and wet grasslands in winter.

Locations: Virtually every moorland area of the Highlands has a population of common gulls as does much of the Border country. Aberdeenshire has the densest population. The largest coastal colony is at Boguille, Isle of Arran, which has over 300 pairs. In England the small colony at Dungeness is the best established one with a maximum of about a dozen pairs. Other pairs or small colonies exist in north Norfolk, the Farnes, in Anglesey and in the northern Pennines.

Passage Migrant and Winter Visitor: Truly huge numbers of common gulls breed in Denmark and Norway and adjacent parts of Scandinavia and Russia. Many move westwards to winter along the coasts of the North Sea, the Channel and the Atlantic. Huge numbers of birds pass through southern England and large numbers stay on to winter. Even ten years ago over 125,000 birds were wintering inland in England alone.

Locations: Lowland reservoirs for roosting birds; playing fields and other grasslands for feeding birds.

Lesser Black-backed Gull *Larus fuscus*

Summer Visitor: This is one of the very few species of gull to leave our shores on a true migration, moving out south-westwards to winter. Most birds arrive in March and depart in September and October, though in some places, particularly in the south, considerable numbers winter. This is a highly colonial bird that, while being predominantly coastal, nevertheless breeds inland in many areas. Some 45,000 pairs breed in Britain, with rather more in England than Scotland. However, over 75% of English birds nest at one huge colony at Walney in Lancashire.

Habitat: Coastal dunes, or flat grassy-topped islets; also high moorlands and large moorland lakes. At other times birds frequent estuaries and marshes, shorelines, playing fields and reservoirs. They tend to feed less frequently on offal and rubbish than other gulls.

Locations: Though it can be seen in many parts of the country, particularly in the north and west, its propensity to form large colonies concentrates birds at the Isles of Scilly, the Skokholm-Skomer area, Flatholm and Steepholm in the Bristol Channel, Anglesey, Walney, and the Isle of May and other Firth of Forth islands. Walney, with 17,500 pairs, is a remarkable site.

Passage Migrant: Lesser black-backed gulls pass through areas where they do not breed in both spring and autumn. During the latter season they may become quite numerous for several weeks and Scandinavian 'black-backed' birds *L. f. fuscus* may be picked out among them.

Grasslands, sewage farms and works, and reservoirs are particularly favoured at such times.
Locations: Everywhere, but less plentiful north of the border.

Herring Gull *Larus argentatus*

Resident: With a population of 280,000 pairs the herring gull is the second most numerous breeding British gull. Though it is most numerous in the north and west, it is catholic in taste and has established colonies even along the comparatively cliff-less coasts of south-east England. It frequently nests inland and can be found breeding in locations as diverse as central London and Sula Sgeir. Walney Island has a huge colony, and no less than 30,000 pairs breed on Anglesey.
Habitat: Sea cliffs, screes, offshore stacks and islands, dunes and marshes, moorlands and increasingly on buildings. Away from its breeding sites it may be found along all sea coasts, in harbours, at rubbish tips, reservoirs and playing fields. Has thrived as a human scavenger.
Locations: During the breeding season can be found along virtually all British coasts; it is the gull that most frequents harbours and every harbour has its own population. Big colonies can be found at Flatholm and Steepholm, Walney, Puffin Island on Anglesey, Calf of Man, Lundy, St Bee's Head, Isle of May, Bass Rock, and particularly along the Aberdeenshire coast.
Winter Visitor: Continental birds move westwards into Britain augmenting the local population particularly along the east and south coasts. Birds found dead should be sub-specifically identified if at all possible.
Locations: The dedicated herring gull-watcher could do no better than watch over the gulls of Teesmouth in mid-winter – though bleak and cold it has 100,000 birds to choose from. The Wash also has good numbers, as do many large inland reservoirs in London and the Midlands.

Iceland Gull *Larus glaucoides*

Winter Visitor: Generally scarce with only a scattering of birds from

November through until April every year. Most are concentrated in the far north, though each year several are noted as far south as the Channel. Seldom seen inland. Can be confused only with much larger glaucous gull.

Habitat: Cliffs and stacks; at other times along shores, harbours, coastal rubbish tips and at other shore-line gull concentration points.

Locations: Regular visitor to Shetland, Outer Hebrides, Scottish north-east and Firth of Clyde. Lerwick and Stornoway in mid-winter are the best bets, though it can be looked for among any large concentration of coastal gulls.

Glaucous Gull *Larus hyperboreus*

Winter Visitor: Rather more common and widespread than similar, but smaller, iceland gull, and ventures further south along the east coast. However, is likewise more numerous in the north, although there are no real concentrations anywhere in Britain.

Habitat: Cliffs and shorelines; in winter frequents shores, harbours and estuaries.

Locations: Regular in Shetland, Orkney and Outer Hebrides. Also among the gull flocks of the north-east and Clyde, and with decreasing frequency in the Humber, Wash and Norfolk coast. Hard winters bring it southward to the Channel coast.

Great Black-backed Gull *Larus marinus*

Resident: In 1970 there were some 22,300 pairs of these large gulls breeding around our coasts of which over 16,000 pairs bred in Scotland. It is, however, found along all rocky coasts, but it only occasionally even attempts to breed between the Firth of Forth and the Isle of Wight. Being much more marine than the other typical British gulls it is not found inland in any great numbers, though it has bred away from the coast in Lancashire, Somerset and Scotland.

Habitat: Rocky sea coasts, particularly with offshore stacks and islets. At other seasons is more pelagic than most other gulls, but also frequents rubbish dumps and reservoirs far inland. Invariably nests at highest point available, sometimes in loose colonies.

Locations: Though the largest British colony of 2,000 pairs is situated at isolated North Rona, there is fortunately no need to travel so far to see these gulls. They can be found along every coastline, though in the south and east these are non-breeding birds. Over half the English population can be found on the Isles of Scilly, while Orkney boasts well over a third of the Scottish total. There are good populations on the Outer Hebrides, Shetland and in Caithness and Sutherland.

Winter Visitor: In winter great black-backed gulls can be found along all coasts and at many of the larger inland reservoirs and rubbish dumps. Some of these visitors come from Norway and Russia, others from Iceland, but most are doubtless British birds.

Locations: Virtually everywhere where water can be found adjacent to food.

Kittiwake *Rissa tridactyla*

Resident: A truly pelagic gull that breeds right around the coasts of Britain, though with a distinct bias toward the rocky and more precipitous coasts of the north and west. About half a million pairs now breed and the population is increasing at a rate of about four per cent per annum. On cliffs it forms dense colonies alongside guillemots, razorbills and puffins.

Habitat: Vertical cliff faces with narrow ledges on which a nest can be lodged; rest of year at sea often well out of sight of land.

Locations: A small colony at The Needles is the furthest east along the Channel coast save for erratic breeding in the North and South Foreland area. Norfolk, Suffolk and Lincolnshire are unsuitable, though there is a colony on Lowestoft Pier. Flamborough Head, to the north, is the southernmost of the east coast cliffs and has over half of the English and Welsh population. Thereafter marvellous cliffs stretch northwards to Shetland with over a quarter of the total British population in Orkney. Outstanding spots are St Abb's Head, Fowlsheugh, Troup and Pennan Heads, Berriedale, Marwick Head, Westray, Papa Westray, Fair Isle and Noss. On the west coast only St Kilda rivals these.

Passage Migrant: Passes along all coasts in large numbers and is occasionally 'wrecked' inland after November storms.

Locations: All coasts with prominent headlands.

Ivory Gull *Pagophila eburnea*

Vagrant: An arctic gull that nests in a scattering of colonies on remote islands and haunts the edge of the pack ice at other times of the year. Unlike Ross's gull, which is of similar habits and habitat, it does move southward with a fair degree of regularity and may then be seen in northernmost Britain.

Habitat: Rocky cliffs and on ground near permanent ice; in winter haunts the edge of the pack ice.

Locations: Turns up from time to time between October and February with increasing frequency the further north. Shetland is most likely location, but Orkney and Outer Hebrides have their fair share. Recent fashion of searching through huge gull concentrations, particularly in north-eastern England, sometimes produces this rare straggler.

Gull-billed Tern *Gelochelidon nilotica*

Summer Visitor: A pair bred at Abberton in 1950 and probably in the previous year. These are the only breeding records of this large, long-winged, gull-like tern.

Habitat: Lakes, marshes, often hawking over dry land, also sea coasts.

Passage Migrant: A scarce double passage migrant that has been identified with much greater regularity in recent years and is now regarded as an annual visitor in small numbers in both spring and autumn. At each season it is most commonly seen at the eastern end of the Channel, presumably indicating that the birds form part of the population that breeds in Denmark. Doubtless this increase of reports is due to the 'sea-watching' fashion that grew up in the 1960s.

Locations: Selsey Bill in Sussex, particularly at the end of April through to June, is the *locus classicus*, but Dungeness, Sandwich Bay and Beachy Head are all good spots. In autumn, passage is quicker and the last week of August and first week of September are the peak times.

Caspian Tern *Sterna caspia*

Passage Migrant: A huge 'sea-tern' with massive head and large coral-red bill that is quite unmistakable. The increase in frequency in recent years to three or four (and up to ten) a year may be due to more intensive watching, but also to an increase in the Scandinavian breeding population. Most reports of mid-summer birds are in July, but there are also records in May, June, August and September.

Habitat: Rocky offshore islands, sand bars, beaches; at other times mostly coastal, but also frequents large rivers.

Locations: Movement is best detected in the Channel region, though some birds evidently turn the corner and move along the coast of East Anglia. Kent, Sussex, Essex, Suffolk and Norfolk are the counties to watch with Minsmere being the favourite spot.

Sandwich Tern *Sterna sandvicensis*

Summer Visitor: Largest of our regular terns and named after the Kentish locality of that name. This is a highly gregarious species that forms dense colonies, with neighbouring pairs sitting within a few inches of one another. It is easily separated from our other terns by size and by the yellow-tipped black bill.

Habitat: Low-lying shingle and sandy islands, or bars in sea. Also islets in marshes.

Locations: Nests here and there around our coasts, but the total for the whole country is less than 10,000 pairs. Of these 2,000 are found on the Farnes and over 4,000 along the north Norfolk coast, almost all at Scolt Head. However, this is a highly erratic species and birds can abandon even a huge colony in a single season. Minsmere and Havergate in Suffolk both have smallish colonies and there is a growing colony in Hampshire. Ravenglass in Cumbria has a good-sized colony. In Scotland most sites are small, though those in the Firth of Forth (Fidra or Inchmickery, not usually both) and at the Sands of Forvie are exceptions.

Passage Migrant: Occurs from mid-March to late October along all shores. Is particularly numerous off Norfolk, Suffolk and the Channel coasts, where it sometimes passes through in substantial numbers.

Locations: Teesmouth, Cley, Benacre Ness, Dungeness, Portland.

Roseate Tern *Sterna dougallii*

Summer Visitor: One of the rarest of British breeding seabirds that arrives later and departs earlier than the other terns. It nests regularly in any numbers at only a handful of colonies, several of which are fortunately nature reserves.

Habitat: Rocky or sandy islands in sea, estuary or even in inland waters. Usually breeds in association with other species of terns.

Locations: In Scotland it is more or less confined to islands in the Firth of Forth (Inchmickery and Fidra) and the Firth of Clyde (Horse Island). In Wales there are two colonies on Anglesey holding 200 pairs between them, and in England there are colonies on the Farnes and Coquet Island. The latter may now be the largest British colony. Elsewhere there are small numbers on the Isles of Scilly. The total population is about 1,500 pairs.

Passage Migrant: Though they pass along most British coasts between April and October, the numbers are very small and it is a matter of chance whether one is encountered or not. Coastal spots offering good feeding near established breeding colonies often have good numbers in late summer.

Locations: North Berwick and westwards in late summer; Bamburgh and Seahouses.

Common Tern *Sterna hirundo*

Summer Visitor: As its name implies this is the most widespread (though perhaps not the most common) of our terns and the basis of starting an identification. It is notoriously difficult to separate from the arctic tern and is often 'lumped' together with that species and called 'comic' tern by bird-watchers. Though the species overlap in range in northern Britain, birds breeding south of a line drawn from Liverpool to Newcastle are most likely to be this species. It is also the more frequent inland.

Habitat: Shallow seas, inlets, estuaries, sand bars and other low-lying coasts; inland on rivers, gravel pits, reservoirs. Outside the breeding season frequents coasts and often seas well out of sight of land.

Locations: Being colonial common terns are of decidedly local distribution. They are more or less absent from the Dee to Portland save for good populations on Anglesey and the Isles of Scilly. They are similarly absent from the Yorkshire coast. Elsewhere there are good colonies along many coasts and inland in the valleys of the Thames, the

Trent and the Fens. Scotland has many colonies including a great many small ones inland. Largest numbers overall can be found on the Farnes; on the North Norfolk coast, as for example at Blakeney Point; at Minsmere; and at Dungeness.

Passage Migrant: To all areas of the country where the common tern does not breed, it is a regular passage migrant. Most pass close inshore along coasts, but truly huge numbers gather at well-known spots to feed.

Locations: South coast watch-outs, e.g. Dungeness, Portland; Teesmouth in late summer; Firth of Forth; Humber; Cley; Minsmere.

Arctic Tern *Sterna paradisaea*

Summer Visitor: Generally arrives a little later and departs a little earlier than its more widespread relative, the common tern. With a handful of exceptions it is confined to northernmost England and Scotland where, however, it is abundant. Though it is seldom seen inland in Britain, it is certainly more numerous than the common tern. A highly vocal and aggressive species in defence of its colonies which are, however, highly prone to disturbance.

Habitat: Rocky and sandy shores, marshes, lake and river banks. Outside breeding season found over open seas, along pack ice and shorelines.

Locations: In England nests in small numbers only in North Norfolk where there are usually some at Blakeney Point; in North Kent; in the Portland-Chesil Beach area; on the Lancashire and Cumbrian coasts as at Ravenglass, Walney and Foulney Island; and in numbers only on Anglesey, the Farnes and nearby Coquet Island. With 3,000 + pairs the Farnes has by far the largest colony. In Scotland it is numerous and widespread with truly huge colonies of perhaps 28,000 pairs shared between Westray and Papa Westray in Orkney – certainly over half of the total for Scotland. A further 7,000 + pairs nest on Shetland.

Passage Migrant: Arctic terns are common passage migrants along coasts south of their breeding range. However, they are often difficult to separate from the similar common terns. Like those birds they often gather at favoured feeding resorts in large numbers.

Locations: Teesmouth, Spurn, North Norfolk, Dungeness Power Station 'Patch', Portland.

Little Tern *Sterna albifrons*

Summer Visitor: A distinctively small tern that is present from mid-April to mid-October and which is essentially coastal in Britain. Elsewhere, even in adjacent Europe, it is found inland along rivers and beside lakes. Though colonial, the birds are always spread out and never form dense packs like Sandwich terns, nor even the more scattered colonies such as those of common terns. A total population of some 1,500 pairs breeds annually.

Habitat: Shingle and sandy seashores, often nesting within a few feet of the mean high water mark. Occasionally inland along rivers and at specially created islands on coastal marshes.

Locations: Largest numbers occur in England with biggest colonies along the North Norfolk coast. Blakeney Point, Scolt Head, Cley Beach all have good numbers. Suffolk (try Minsmere), Essex, Kent (Dungeness), Sussex (Rye Harbour) and Dorset are also good. Farther north the Farnes, the Firth of Forth, the Uists and Benbecula in the Outer Hebrides, Walney and Anglesey all have good populations. Unfortunately disturbance is a major threat to the little tern.

Passage Migrant: The little tern occurs on all coasts as a migrant.
Locations: Non-specific away from breeding colonies.

Whiskered Tern *Chlidonias hybridus*

Passage Migrant: An extremely scarce bird of passage that occurs once or more almost every year, but which may be becoming more frequent of late. It is a 'marsh' tern that feeds by picking food from the surface of inland waters and that is extremely numerous in many parts of its range, which is distinctly southern in western Europe.

Habitat: Marshes and lakes, often well away from the coast and with a strong growth of emergent vegetation. Particularly numerous on rice fields.

Locations: Most British records occur in spring and are heavily biased toward the south-west indicating over-shooting rather than passage of eastern breeding birds. Large waters such as lowland reservoirs in southern counties are the best places to search, May and June being the best months. There is a much smaller passage of birds in late August and September in Channel counties.

Black Tern *Chlidonias niger*

Summer Visitor: An extremely rare breeding bird with just the occasional pair nesting in East Anglia. Generally common and widespread on the Continent of Europe eastwards into Russia as well as in North America. The typical 'marsh' tern feeds predominantly on insects picked in flight from the surface of water.
Habitat: Lakes, reservoirs, marshes as well as salt pans and sea coasts on passage.
Locations: The only published location is the Ouse Washes where pairs bred in the late 1960s and have occasionally done so since.
Passage Migrant: A widespread passage migrant in spring and autumn in southern England. Spring passage is generally fast and more or less confined to mid-May. On the large Midland and London reservoirs, where the birds are regular, 12th May is an excellent date, though some pass through a little later as well. In autumn many marshes and reservoirs hold these birds for several weeks.
Locations: Grafham, Rutland, Eyebrook, Barn Elms, Staines, Queen Mother, Weir Wood, Chew and other large inland waters. Also Cley, Minsmere and the Ouse Washes.

White-winged Black Tern *Chlidonias leucopterus*

Passage Migrant: A scarce passage migrant that has either become more numerous or, more likely, has been more frequently identified over the past twenty years. Generally similar to both black and whiskered terns in autumn, though sufficiently distinct to create few problems for the competent field observer given good views. Predominantly eastern European in distribution.
Habitat: Inland waters, lakes, marshes, floods, salt pans, sometimes coastal.
Locations: Is far more numerous (almost three times) in autumn than in spring, and in both seasons occurs in southern and eastern England from Lincolnshire to Avon. Reservoirs and floods in Kent and Sussex such as Stodmarsh and Weir Wood are likely spots, as is the new Bewl Bridge.

Guillemot *Uria aalge*

Resident: Guillemots are the most common and widespread members of the seabird communities for which Britain is so justly famous. Along the cliffs that line so much of our northern and western coasts, ledges are packed with guillemots, razorbills, kittiwakes and fulmars, while small parties of puffins sit about apparently unconcerned and unmoved by the activity that surrounds them. One could be forgiven, when faced with such abundance, for thinking that these must be the most numerous British birds, but one would be wrong. Guillemots are in such decline, due almost entirely to oil pollution of the seas, that it must be considered a race between the extinction of the species and the running out of oil. Britain has some of the world's best seabird cliffs, and the responsibility for their survival.

Habitat: Steep sea cliffs with ledges; outside breeding season at sea but usually within sight of land or in the continental shelf.

Locations: There are no colonies in the south and east of England between The Needles and Bempton. Those in the south-west are fast declining and north of Flamborough there are none until the Farnes and the Scottish border. Wales has some excellent colonies on its islands, the most easily visited one being at Skomer. North-east Scotland has some very large colonies and the coast of Caithness is virtually one gigantic seabird colony. Orkney and Shetland are full of guillemots, but the largest colonies of all are at St. Kilda and the Flannans. Top spots easily accessible are Handa with 30,000 pairs; Fowlsheugh; Marwick 25,000 + ; Noss; Duncansby; Bempton 12,500; Lundy 1,500.

Winter Visitor: Most guillemots remain near their breeding sites throughout the year, but some birds move away and can be seen around our coasts in small numbers.

Locations: None specific.

Razorbill *Alca torda*

Resident: The distribution of razorbills around our coasts coincides more or less exactly with that of the more numerous guillemot, even though the two have quite distinct breeding niches. While the guillemot lines the open cliffs, one bird pressed tight against the next, the razorbill

Top **Knot** pack together at the famous Hilbre Island high tide roost on the Cheshire Dee. Favoured estuaries may have huge numbers of this chunky dunlin-like bird in winter, while other seemingly suitable areas nearby are totally ignored.
Bottom Pelagic trips, so popular in the United States for example, are surprisingly ignored by British watchers. They can, however, reveal spectacular concentrations of seabirds such as **fulmars, great shearwaters** seen here with a **sooty shearwater.**

Top The lack of a male has resulted in the demise of the tiny breeding population of **snowy owls** on the Shetland island of Fetlar, though several females are still present throughout the year. This is their only regular British site.

Bottom Once reduced to a handful of pairs in an obscure part of central Wales, the **red kite** has slowly increased and spread to other parts of that country. This juvenile has been wing-tagged as part of a scientific study.

occupies niches and crannies among the more broken cliff areas where it is, of course, much more difficult to find and count. Large colonies are thus, to say the least, elusive, but there are many places around our shores where razorbills can be seen in good numbers.

Habitat: Sea-cliff cracks and crannies; outside breeding season found at sea, usually at no great distance from land.

Locations: As with the guillemot there is only one colony, at Bempton, between the Farnes and The Needles. The Welsh islands have decent populations, but it is only in Scotland that the species is really numerous – Orkney and Caithness are outstandingly rich. Top spots with really strong colonies are at Handa, with 8,000 pairs; Noss 3,000; Ailsa Craig 2,300; Skomer 1,500; Fair Isle 1,200.

Winter Visitor: Widespread at sea, razorbills can be seen from most parts of the British coast in small numbers throughout the winter.

Locations: None specific.

Black Guillemot *Cepphus grylle*

Resident: An attractive black and white auk that is more or less confined to Scotland where it is resident and, therefore, unknown to those not familiar with its breeding grounds. It is nowhere as abundant as, say, the guillemot or puffin, preferring instead to breed in small groups scattered thinly over suitable habitat. It nests in deep crevices among the boulder screes formed at the bases of sheer cliffs where it is very difficult to observe. Most black guillemots, or 'tysties' as they are called in Scotland, are thus seen at sea below the cliffs where they are easily picked out among the guillemots, razorbills and puffins that nest among the higher levels of the sea cliff tenements. The birds are, however, remarkably adaptable and will nest in rabbit burrows, piles of wood, in caves and blow holes, and even in piers and ruins some distance from the sea.

Habitat: Crevices at base of sea cliffs; outside breeding season at sea near breeding colonies, occasionally moving to other coasts.

Locations: Outside Scotland there are colonies in northern and eastern Anglesey, the Isle of Man and St Bee's Head. North of the border the species is widespread in north and west, but almost absent in the east south of Caithness. About 8,000 pairs breed in total with highest numbers, over 300 pairs, at Auskerry in Orkney. Shetland and Fair Isle have good numbers as do the Monarch Isles in the Outer Hebrides.

Little Auk *Alle alle*

Winter Visitor: Though no more than a scattering of little auks reach Britain every year, and though it breeds at only a handful of high arctic colonies, it is nevertheless a candidate for the title of the world's most numerous bird. Where it is found, numbers are beyond description. Like starlings going to roost they fly against the sky, wheeling this way and that, wings whirring as they come in to land on some rocky promontary often some distance from the sea. The nearest colonies to Britain are at Jan Mayen, and eastern and southern Greenland. There is a small colony in northern Iceland at Grimsey, but this totters on the verge of extinction.

Habitat: Arctic screes; outside breeding season at sea along the edge of the pack ice.

Locations: Small numbers visit northernmost Britain from November to February and may then be looked for off the coasts of Shetland. At irregular intervals they move southwards along the east coast as far as Norfolk where sheer persistence of observation frequently produces the odd individual. Elsewhere they are known only as storm-driven waifs, but their vulnerability to winter gales has brought them to almost every part of Britain on occasion. Sometimes 'wrecks' will produce birds in the most unlikely of places.

Puffin *Fratercula arctica*

Resident: The colourful and often comical puffin is the North Atlantic representative of a genus that has its origins and is far more numerous in the Bering Straits of the North Pacific. Britain is almost at the southern limit of its range, but also has some of the very largest colonies. Over the years there has been quite a definite decline in numbers with colonies in southern England slowly disappearing one by one and even the huge Scottish puffinries entering a serious decline. However, the Scottish situation seems to have been somewhat over exaggerated due more to the difficulties inherent in counting puffins than to any other factor. Certainly the numbers on Lundy, once called 'Isle of Puffins', have declined from 3,500 in 1939 to less than 50 by 1969.

The causes of this decline remain obscure for puffins only figure small in deaths due to oil spills.

Habitat: Grassy slopes in and atop sea-cliffs, usually in association with other cliff-nesting seabirds; outside breeding season at sea but often near breeding sites.

Locations: Only one colony (at Bempton) between The Needles and Coquet Island. Decidedly thin on south coast, i.e. at The Needles, Durston Head, Portland Bill. Isles of Scilly and Lundy have good colonies as do a couple of spots in north Cornwall. Really substantial colonies at Skomer and Skokholm, a few small ones in Anglesey, Isle of Man and St Bee's Head. There are good numbers on the Farnes and on the islands of the Firth of Forth. Large colonies exist around the coasts of Scotland with outstanding ones at St Kilda, Shiants, Fair Isle, Unst, Foula, Sule and Stack Skerry. Of these Fair Isle and Unst must be regarded as the most accessible, but Caithness is even more available and has plenty of birds.

Winter Visitor: Puffins can be found in very small numbers along most shores in winter, though they seldom come in close enough for satisfactory identification unless storm-driven.

Locations: None specific.

Rock Dove *Columba livia*

Resident: While feral stocks descended from this species are among the most successful of all birds, inhabiting almost every city centre over large areas of the world, the genuine wild rock dove has become a considerable rarity throughout its range. This apparent dichotomy is explained by the fact that feral birds have, more or less everywhere, returned to their original habitat and mated freely with the wild birds they find there. The stock is thus mixed and truly wild birds disappear. The truly wild rock dove is a cliff breeder and birds approximating to the wild type can be found along most suitable British coasts; most are feral.

Habitat: Sea cliffs.

Locations: Wild rock doves can be found only along the coasts of northern and western Scotland between Kintyre and the Isle of Arran and north-eastern Caithness. There are a few in southern Orkney, in the Outer Hebrides, but not in Shetland.

Stock Dove *Columba oenas*

Resident: Stock doves are most generally seen in agricultural areas where a good growth of trees, either in hedgerows or old woodlands, provides them with nesting holes. They are easily confused with feral pigeons which exhibit such a range of different plumages, but always lack white on the rump and black bars on the wing. In country districts they take readily to nest boxes erected specially for them and will even occupy those in large gardens.

Habitat: Farmland with old trees, but also nests in cliffs and quarries.

Locations: Expanded range northwards and westwards over past 100 years and are now found as far north as the Great Glen. They are, however, decidedly scarce in the Highlands, parts of the Border Hills, the Lake District and the Welsh hills. Most commonly found in southern and eastern England in small flocks on the plough.

Woodpigeon *Columba palumbus*

Resident: Three to four million pairs of woodpigeons nest in Britain making this one of the country's most numerous and successful birds. Like similar and closely related species found in other parts of the world, it was formerly a bird of deciduous woodland. Today it is the most important avian agricultural pest and uses trees and woods only to nest and roost. Over the past 200 years woodpigeons have multiplied and spread to virtually every part of the country. They feed on fallen grain, on sown seeds, on root and other crops, and do immense damage. Yet at the same time as the inevitable war was started on the species, man was planting more and larger forests that acted as highly effective woodpigeon nurseries. So numerous and successful did it become that during the present century it has moved into large urban areas and has even adapted to nesting on buildings in London.

Habitat: Agricultural land with nearby trees, hedgerows or woodland; also city centres and pure woodland.

Locations: Nests everywhere save the highest mountain regions of Scotland.

Collared Dove *Streptopelia decaocto*

Resident: The first collared doves arrived in Britain to breed in Norfolk in 1955. Within 25 years some 30,000 pairs were breeding and they were considered a pest in many areas. This dramatic ornithological event is merely a stage in the expansion of the range of this species which began in the 1930's from its origins in south-east Europe. It has now reached the Faeroes and seems set to find its way to the New World in due course. It is even possible that it may eventually reach the prairies of North America to take the place of the extinct passenger pigeon with possibly disastrous results for mankind.

Habitat: Parks and gardens with conifers and spilt grain; most numerous in coastal districts.

Locations: Most numerous in south and east becoming thinner on the ground towards the north and west. Absent from hill and mountain districts, scarce in Shetland. Wildfowl parks, with their plentiful grain supplies and spirit of at least tolerance towards all birds, are ideal for collared doves: try Slimbridge and Peakirk where the Wildfowl Trust supports hundreds of these birds. Ramsgate has a huge population said to keep hotel visitors awake at night!

Turtle Dove *Streptopelia turtur*

Summer Visitor: One of the most attractive and beautiful of all British birds, the turtle dove is a summer visitor that is normally present from mid-April to the end of October. Despite extreme pressure of shooting in the Mediterranean region, the species has increased and spread northwards in (ornithological) historical times and continues to do so. Its growing population is undoubtedly due to changing agricultural techniques providing ploughed land where its main food plant, fumitory, thrives, but it also gathers at spilt grain and may then associate with resident collared doves and stay on later than normal in their company.

Habitat: Hedgerows on agricultural land, particularly arable.

Locations: Widespread over most of England save the south-west, the Pennines, the north, and large urban sprawls. Absent from most of Wales and Scotland, though individuals do overshoot in spring.

Cuckoo *Cuculus canorus*

Summer Visitor: One of only two species of brood parasites to have colonized Europe and the only one to occur regularly in Britain. The species' familiar 'cuck-oo' call has made it as familiar to townsman as countryman, and a symbol of the arrival of spring. Yet it is not a familiar bird, doubtless often being mistaken for a hawk or kestrel and, in any case, being somewhat secretive and elusive in habit. The cuckoo is a remarkably adaptable bird occupying a huge range of habitats. It is able to achieve such a range by virtue of finding suitable hosts for its eggs and young, which vary from reed warblers among the swamps to meadow pipits on the high moorland tops. Each individual bird specializes and produces eggs that bear a marked similarity to those of its host.

Habitat: Catholic from marshes, woodlands, hedgerows to mountains and moorland.

Locations: Present from mid-April to the end of August in every part of Britain. Slightly thinner on the ground in parts of the Highlands.

Barn Owl *Tyto alba*

Resident: One of the most widespread of all the world's birds with a cosmopolitan distribution that takes it to all continents. The species never reaches further north than Britain, though it is rare or absent in northernmost Scotland in the Highland region. However, it has declined over most of Britain throughout this century and was one of the species hardest hit by the pesticide disaster of the 1950s and 1960s. It is still thoughtlessly destroyed by shooting in many country districts and is also a common road casualty. As a result, nowhere is it common or easy to see.

Habitat: Agricultural land with hedges and dells and areas of waste; nests in barns, holes in trees, cliff holes, etc.

Locations: Absent only from Highland Scotland, and the Pennines and other hill districts. Thinly spread elsewhere with a population of between 3,000 and 8,000 pairs. Best watched for in suitable habitats at dusk in the south-west, south Wales, the north-west and southern Scotland.

Snowy Owl *Nyctea scandiaca*

Resident: In June 1967 the first snowy owl nest ever found in Britain was discovered on the Shetland island of Fetlar. It was immediately protected by the RSPB and a round-the-clock guard system ensured that young owlets were raised. Since then the birds and their (presumed) descendants have bred irregularly at this site and have spread to summer and winter elsewhere in Shetland. Breeding is never certain with these birds and the lack of a strong male may well prove to be the species' undoing as a British colonist. Otherwise the snowy owl is a rare vagrant to Britain and mainland Scotland and is even rarer further south. Like so many arctic species its numbers tend to be cyclical and its pattern of movements irruptive.

Habitat: Arctic tundra; at other times and, in Britain, frequents high moorland and open landscapes.

Locations: Snowy owls are still regular only on the island of Fetlar and, though individuals have wintered in the Cairngorms, at Fair Isle and elsewhere in Shetland, this island offers by far the best chance of seeing the species.

Little Owl *Athene noctua*

Resident: Introduced at many spots in the middle and latter part of last century, it was not until 1900 or so that the little owl really started to spread and colonize Britain. Today it numbers in excess of 10,000 pairs and has probably suffered a slight decline since the 1950s. It is abroad in daylight and is always about in the early evening when there is still sufficient light to facilitate observation. It also has the endearing habit of sitting atop prominent perches such as telegraph posts and wires, where it is easily seen. It feeds mainly on small birds, though worms, beetles and snails also figure in its diet. Elsewhere it breeds right across Eurasia to northern China and southwards into North Africa and Saudi Arabia.

Habitat: Agricultural land with hedgerows, waste ground, quarries, gorges, parkland.

Locations: This owl is widespread in England, but almost totally absent from Scotland, from many parts of Wales and from the upland areas of the Lake District, the Pennines, Dartmoor, Exmoor and the Yorkshire Moors. The more broken the landscape with hills and hedgerows the more likely the occurrence of little owls.

Tawny Owl *Strix aluco*

Resident: The tawny, or 'brown owl' as country people occasionally still call it, is a widespread resident in Britain and, with a population in excess of 50,000 pairs, is the most numerous of British owls. It nests mainly in tree holes, though it will also use holes in old buildings as well as specially erected nest boxes. This choice of nest site is clearly responsible for the only gaps in its British distribution, in the Highlands and Islands of Scotland and in the fenland district of East Anglia. It is also absent from the Isle of Man and from Ireland. Elsewhere its familiar 'Whoo-who-who' call announces its unseen presence as does a sharp 'kee-wick'. Both are most frequently uttered in late autumn when territories are being re-established prior to late winter breeding. In central London these owls have abandoned a diet of small mammals in favour of the more abundant house sparrow with considerable success and can now be found in the very heart of the city.

Habitat: Open areas with deciduous woods and hedgerows, city centres and suburbs.

Locations: With the exceptions mentioned above where trees are thinly spread or absent tawny owls may be listened for throughout Britain. They respond well to nest boxes for those who wish to see more of them, but may attack those who disturb their nests.

Long-eared Owl *Asio otus*

Resident: This is the most nocturnal of British owls and, as a result, the most difficult to see. It seldom hunts even in twilight and is notoriously difficult to flush either from its roost or nest. As a result, our knowledge of the species' distribution is certainly imperfect and only a guess, of some 2,000 to 7,000 pairs, can be made at its population. It inhabits mostly coniferous woods where it occupies the old nests of crows and magpies, but will also move into deciduous woodland in the absence of tawny owls as, for instance, on the Isle of Man. It can be located by listening for its hooting call early in the New Year or for the strangely eerie call of the young of mid-summer.

Habitat: Mainly coniferous woods and plantations, old coverts, and deciduous woods in various parts of the country.

Locations: There is a quite definite concentration of long-eared owls in the northern and eastern part of the country; also along the Suffolk coast, in the Brecks, along the Yorkshire part of the Trent, in the forests north of Solway, in eastern Aberdeenshire and on the Black Isle between Cromarty and Beauly Firths; and any coniferous forest in central and eastern England. A pair regularly inhabits Stornoway Woods in Lewis.

Short-eared Owl *Asio flammeus*

Resident: An open country owl that frequently hunts during the day and quarters the ground in the manner of a harrier in its search for voles. Like the predators of the arctic its numbers are totally dependent on the population level of its prey and thus fluctuate enormously. It is mainly a moorland bird, but will occupy any area of open land that is not disturbed. It can thus be found on heaths and marshes, and in young plantations even in lowland districts of Britain.

Habitat: Moors, marshes, heaths and other undisturbed open landscapes.

Locations: Though it is widely spread throughout Britain save for southern and central England where suitable habitat is difficult to find, there are particular areas in which short-eared owls find an ideal niche. Among others are Sheppey, The Wash, the northern Pennines and particularly the Border country, Caithness and Orkney. In these areas they are often remarkably numerous and easily seen.

Winter Visitor: An influx of winter visitors from overseas as well as southward movements of our own populations often build up considerable winter concentrations at favoured east coast marshes.

Locations: The Wash, North Norfolk, Breydon, Orford, Dengie and Foulness, Sheppey, North Kent.

Nightjar *Caprimulgus europaeus*

Summer Visitor: Nightjars arrive in Britain from Africa from late April onwards, but are seldom present in numbers until late May. They depart again by late August though some birds remain until the end of September. They are essentially crepuscular, hunting only during the periods of dawn and dusk and spending the day in well-camouflaged hiding. To see a nightjar thus requires a special expedition to suitable habitat at the right time of the day. Then they may be heard at considerable distances as they produce their characteristic 'churring' note that is often prolonged for several minutes. Having established the presence of 'singing' birds the secret is to position oneself with a view of as much sky as possible, avoid midges and mosquito attacks, and keep one's eyes peeled for a soundless flying bird with the silhouette of a kestrel. A 'ku-ick' call note or a wing-clapping display often help to draw attention to a flying bird. Nightjars are immensely curious and will approach, fly round and enchant a fortunate observer.

Habitat: Dry sandy heaths with scattered trees, commons, clearings in forests, downland, shingle banks, open moorland.

Locations: Nightjars have quite definitely declined in numbers in recent years and are now decidedly scarce in many areas. Their stronghold remains southern England and East Anglia, but they are thinly spread northwards to southern Scotland and, more rarely, to Inverness and beyond. They are often found near chalk and sandy heaths. Good spots are North Norfolk, the Brecks, the east Suffolk heaths, the Surrey Commons, the New Forest and Dorset heaths.

Swift *Apus apus*

Summer Visitor: Swifts arrive at the end of April and throughout May. They are highly aerial birds that may be mistaken for swallows or martins, but they have decidedly longer wings than those birds and are all black in colour. They are the most aerial of all birds spending their nights asleep on the wing, gathering nesting material and preening in the air, and even mating while flying. They inhabit towns and suburbs where they are obvious as they scream in small parties over the roof tops. Some birds are still found nesting in cliffs, doubtless their original habitat, but man has done much to increase the world population of this highly attractive bird. With a few notable exceptions swifts can be seen virtually every day between mid-May and mid-August anywhere in Britain.

Habitat: Nests in holes under eaves and natural cavities in cliffs; mostly found in small towns and suburbs of large cities, seldom in villages or isolated houses.
Locations: Absent only from the Highlands and Islands and some parts of the Border country.

Kingfisher *Alcedo atthis*

Resident: One of the most colourful of British birds and known to virtually every inhabitant of these islands. However the kingfisher is not particularly numerous and is absent from large areas that might be assumed to be suitable. It is generally seen as a flash of bright cobalt blue as it disappears along some narrow river or stream, but it is equally at home along canals, the shores of ponds and lakes, mountain streams and even quite narrow ditches. Being totally dependent on small fish, particularly bullheads, it is particularly vulnerable to bad winters and its numbers may be decimated by a severe freeze-up. At such times it may even turn up on coastal marshes in its search for open water.
Habitat: Streams, rivers, ponds, gravel-pits, marshes.
Locations: Kingfishers are widespread in southern, eastern and central England and in Wales. They are more localized in the north and east, and in Scotland are decidedly scarce, becoming progressively more so further north. They are usually chanced upon rather than searched for.

Hoopoe *Upupa epops*

Summer Visitor: The hoopoe is a widespread species that breeds over huge areas of the Old World, and which only rarely comes to Britain and even more rarely stays on to breed. It comes here mainly as a result of spring overshooting and can be sought from mid-March onwards, though its distinctive call, from which it is named, draws attention to its presence. It frequents short grass and is as liable to turn up in an orchard or garden as in a wood; in general it is a confiding species with a high level of tolerance towards humans.
Habitat: Open woodlands, parks, gardens, orchards.
Locations: Southern England from Cornwall to Kent is the most likely

area to see a hoopoe, and late April to May the most likely period. Sussex has as many breeding records as any other part of the country.

Wryneck *Jynx torquilla*

Summer Visitor: Once a common sound of the English spring, the call of the wryneck has disappeared from much of the countryside over the past 150 years. This decline has been variously attributed to climatic amelioration, a decline in food supplies, agricultural pesticides, habitat destruction and so on; now, it is generally agreed that wrynecks are all but extinct in England. However, what England has lost Scotland has gained, for wrynecks have started breeding there since the 1960s and are now more numerous in the north than the south. There can be little doubt that these new arrivals are of Scandinavian origin. Wrynecks are best looked for during the two or three weeks of late April when their 'quee-quee-quee' calls can be heard. Once they have laid eggs they remain silent. At other times they are scarce autumn migrants, mainly to the east coast.

Habitat: Open woodland, parks, gardens: in Scotland among open conifer and birch forests.

Locations: Surrey heaths, Dorset heaths, Kent orchards; in the north the Spey Valley woodlands.

Green Woodpecker *Picus viridis*

Resident: The loud, far-carrying 'yaffling' call of the green woodpecker is a familiar sound over most parts of the English and Welsh countryside. The species requires woods in which to breed, but forages much over open ground, where it finds ants (its favourite prey) usually on the ground. It is thus most numerous in parkland where the particular combination of trees and open ground suits it perfectly. Prior to 1945 this woodpecker was completely absent from Scotland and parts of northern England. Within 20 years it had colonized the Lake District, the Border country and as far north as Loch Lomond. Today it has spread into the southern Highlands as far north as Aberdeen.

Habitat: Open woodland, parks, gardens.

Locations: Most numerous in southern England and Wales where its characteristic call draws attention to it. Absent from the Fens (no trees), from parts of northern England, and from Scotland from the Grampians northwards (but liable to turn up soon).

Great Spotted Woodpecker
Dendrocopus major

Resident: The most common and widespread woodpecker in Britain. About 30,000 pairs of great spotted woodpeckers breed in the woodlands of Britain where they have a foraging niche more or less to themselves. On the Continent of Europe a host of closely related species compete for food and living space. In spring, and occasionally at other times, great spotted woodpeckers 'drum' on dead branches to produce a hollow sound that echoes through the woods and draws attention to their presence. Like other woodpeckers they have a deeply undulating, bouncy flight that makes them easy to identify.
Habitat: Deciduous and coniferous woodland, also parks and even gardens.
Locations: Absent from the Fens and from parts of the Highlands and extreme north of Scotland. The habit of coming to bird tables to feed on kitchen scraps has made it easier to locate throughout the country.

Lesser Spotted Woodpecker
Dendrocopus minor

Resident: A widespread species that is not uncommon, but which remains decidedly difficult to locate and see. It 'drums' like other woodpeckers, but for a less prolonged period and at a higher pitch; it inhabits the canopy rather than the main trunk and limbs of trees; and it nests higher than other woodpeckers. It is also remarkably self-effacing and many bird-watchers go for years at a time without seeing one.
Habitat: Parkland, orchards, lines of alders, copses.
Locations: Confined to England and Wales, though recent records in Perthshire may indicate the beginning of a colonization from Scandinavia. Very evenly spread through the country, but with a concentration perhaps in the home counties.

Woodlark *Lullula arborea*

Resident: The woodlark almost qualifies as one of only a handful of birds that are confined to Europe: it does, however, extend into North Africa and eastwards along the southern shore of the Caspian. In Britain it has always been right on the very edge of its range and recent years have seen an alarming decline in its fortunes. As recently as the early 1950s it was a regular breeder in Lincolnshire and bred irregularly in Yorkshire. Today it is regular only in southernmost England, with a total population of less than 450 pairs. This decline closely parallels that of the red-backed shrike and wryneck, two other birds of open scrubby country. However, the population and distribution of this attractive bird is notoriously prone to change and we can hope that its fortunes will rise once more. Though similar to the skylark, its habitat, habit of perching freely, and pattern of pale eyebrows that meet at the rear of the crown are diagnostic.

Habitat: Dry heaths and commons with scattered trees or other perches.

Locations: Only a handful of places can be considered regular woodlark haunts: the Brecks, Surrey Commons, New Forest, and the heaths and commons of southern Dartmoor. It is virtually pointless to search north of a line joining the Severn to The Wash.

Skylark *Alauda arvensis*

Resident: The song of the skylark is almost as noted as that of the nightingale though, one could venture, for very different reasons. Whereas the nightingale is a nocturnal virtuoso, the skylark is a positive herald of dawn, the earliest songster in virtually every part of its range. Thus the expression to be 'up with the lark' is actually true. It hovers high in the air, apparently singing the whole day away. Extending from Spain right across Eurasia as far as Japan, the skylark is a very successful species. It occupies a huge range of habitats and is the most widespread of all British birds. A population of some 3 million might be about right.

Habitat: Open country from meadows and ploughland to marsh and moor, from sea level to the highest mountain tops.

Locations: Present in every part of Britain more or less throughout the year. A difficult bird to miss.

Winter Visitor: Numbers of skylarks enter the country in October and mingle with our native birds: they nearly all leave by April.

Locations: None required.

Shore Lark *Eremophila alpestris*

Winter Visitor: Though it may be a 'shore' lark in Britain, elsewhere over its huge range it occupies quite different habitats and would undoubtedly far better be called 'horned lark' as it is in North America. Its distribution is quite extraordinary. It breeds in the far north with a circumpolar range that extends southwards throughout the whole of North America. In the Old World, in contrast, its distribution in the north is separated by more than a thousand miles from a southerly range that extends from the Atlas Mountains of Morocco to the Himalayas. However, to Britain, despite breeding to the north and south, it remains a distinctly scarce winter visitor, mainly to the east coast.

Habitat: Arctic tundra, alpine wastes; in winter frequents open areas such as shingle beaches and sand dunes. Very rarely ventures far from the shore.

Locations: From Lincolnshire to Kent: Gibraltar Point, Cley and Blakeney, Walberswick, Sheppey.

Sand Martin *Riparia riparia*

Summer Visitor: There can be no doubt that this attractive little hirundine has benefitted considerably from the changes that humans have wrought to the landscape of Britain, particularly during the present century. The creation and exploitation of sand pits has developed soft cliffs in areas that were formerly devoid of sand martin habitat. Unfortunately, though this must have increased the numbers of martins very significantly, the recent drought at the southern edge of the Sahara has cut the population possibly by as much as two-thirds or even three-quarters. Today sand martins are still widespread but they are not as numerous as they were even 10 years ago. Being colonial and

gregarious at all stages of their lives they have proved an ideal subject for intensive ringing studies. Present from April through to September. *Habitat:* Sandy cliffs often near sea; inland at both functioning and disused sand pits.
Locations: The patchy distribution of the sand martin reflects the underlying geological formations as well as that of any bird. It is largely absent from chalk areas, high moorlands and the Scottish Outer Hebrides, Orkneys and Shetlands. Its habit of roosting communally with swallows in large reed beds on migration opens up other areas worth searching.

Swallow *Hirundo rustica*

Summer Visitor: Though swallows have been recorded as early as 4 February and as late as New Year's Eve, they are a sign of summer that is every bit as poignant as the first call of the cuckoo. They arrive in numbers in mid-April and are then present well into October. In America, where the same species is found, they are called 'barn swallows' to differentiate them from the many other species of hirundines. This is a particularly apt name, for throughout its range the species is as dependent on man-built structures as any bird. Old sheds, barns, garages, disused houses are all pressed into service.
Habitat: Virtually universal and nests wherever suitable structures can be found. The outskirts of villages seem to have a particular attraction.
Locations: Apart from Shetland, Orkney, the Outer Hebrides, and the more desolate and wild parts of the Highlands, the swallow is universally distributed throughout the country. Perhaps half a million pairs breed in an average year. On passage huge numbers may gather to roost in reed beds with sand martins.

House Martin *Delichon urbica*

Summer Visitor: With its ready colonization from presumably the earliest times of man's living and working constructions, the house martin must have increased and spread dramatically in recent years. The growth of towns, and particularly of surburban areas, has provided the species with a completely new environment where formerly it was dependent on cliffs for nest sites. Now a limiting factor is the availability of mud for nest construction in an age that seems preoccupied with tidying up virtually everything. House martins, with their under-the-eaves domed nests and bold white rumps, are quite unmistakable. They are present from mid-April to October.

Habitat: Suburbs rather than city centres; eaves of houses, flats, water towers, and, in some places still, cliffs – the original nest site.

Locations: Widely distributed throughout the country and absent only from the highest hills. Also very scarce in Shetland, Orkney, and the Inner and Outer Hebrides.

Richard's Pipit *Anthus novaeseelandiae*

Vagrant: Best categorized as a 'vagrant' although there are now so many records of Richard's pipits every autumn that it will soon merit 'passage migrant' status. It is a large, well-streaked pipit with long legs and bold upright stance that has, as its scientific name implies, a distribution that extends as far as the Antipodes. In many parts of the world it is quite common. Its new-found status in Britain may be due to a population increase, or a change in migrational direction. However, it seems much more likely to be due to a growth in expertise among those bird-watchers whose main aim is to see scarce birds. Once learned its sparrow-like 'churrup' is unmistakable and the easiest method of locating the species.

Habitat: Grassland, margins of fields, roadsides, lawns.

Locations: Though vagrant Richard's pipits may turn up anywhere, there is a distinct concentration along the south and east coasts of England and in Shetland. Best spots are Spurn, Gibraltar Point, Wells and Holkham, Cley, Isles of Scilly and Shetland, but an observer who knows this bird will find it in all manner of places from mid-September to the first week in November.

Tree Pipit *Anthus trivialis*

Summer Visitor: Tree pipits arrive in Britain from late March onwards, though numbers are generally low until mid-April; they stay through to September. Though superficially similar to the more common and widespread meadow pipit, this species is more brown than olive, and always appears cleaner and more distinctly marked. However, its choice of habitat, which always contains bushes, small trees or telegraph wires from which to sing, is characteristic as, indeed, is its song flight with its parachute-like descent.

Habitat: Heaths, scrub, open woodland, felled areas, parks, all with suitable 'song posts'.

Locations: Present from Sutherland to Kent, but a strangely patchy breeding distribution with absences from considerable areas such as western Cornwall, Caithness, much of Suffolk and Norfolk (as well as the more easily explained Fen district), and large parts of western Scotland. Is abundant in the Weald, in Wales and in western Scotland.

Meadow Pipit *Anthus pratensis*

Resident: Although it is confined to northern Europe and adjacent parts of the western Palearctic region, with but a small outpost in the New World on the east coast of Greenland, the meadow pipit is a remarkably successful bird. It can be found on marshes below sea level, but is just as much at home on the highest mountain tops; indeed the only crucial factor seems to be open ground. Its characteristic thin 'seet' call serves to identify it along coasts during passage periods and in winter, an essential feature that saves time examining every pipit in the search for a rarity. Occasionally, really huge numbers occur on passage and in excess of two million pairs probably breed.

Habitat: Open landscapes from coasts, marshes, estuaries and floods, to high screes and mountain plateaux.

Locations: Absent only from the most densely wooded areas of Britain in the Midlands, East Anglia and the Weald. Large numbers along coasts in autumn and winter.

Rock Pipit / Water Pipit
Anthus spinoletta

Resident: Rock pipits are not difficult to identify as such. However, they do vary quite considerably not only in plumage, but also in habitat. These variations are regarded as quite distinct sub-species and receive a Latin trinomial. They are identifiable in the field as quite separate birds, although only two sub-species receive the full accolade of a vernacular name:

Anthus spinoletta petrosus (Rock Pipit) breeds around the coasts of Britain and north-west France.

Anthus spinoletta spinoletta (Water Pipit) breeds in the mountains of southern and central Europe from Spain to the Carpathians, but winters in the lowlands and is found in southern England.

Anthus spinoletta littoralis (Scandinavian Rock Pipit) breeds along the coasts of Scandinavia and the Baltic eastwards.

Each of these birds is found in Britain, though only the rock pipit *A.s. petrosus* breeds here.

Habitat: Coasts, especially rocky or broken areas with sheltered gullies, never far from the shore.

Locations: All rocky coasts from Flamborough northwards to Scotland and from the Isle of Wight westwards. Absent from south and east save for a few in Sussex, and from Lancashire.

Winter Visitor: Two distinct sub-species join our native birds in winter. The Scandinavian rock pipit is always browner than our bird, and the water pipit is always more grey. The former occurs on the east and south coasts from October and November onwards; the latter winters in southern England at reservoirs and watercress beds.

Locations: None regular.

Yellow Wagtail *Motacilla flava*

Summer Visitor: Present in Britain from mid-April to September, this widespread species is regarded as being in a state of 'evolutionary flux'. Impressive as such a term may be, in simple language it means that the species has developed a range of quite distinct sub-species any of which may soon become full species in the course of evolution. Yellow wagtails are characterized by different coloured heads and by different head patterns, and it is the searching out of these, rather than observing the species as such, that provides bird-watching sport. Each of these sub-species receives, of course, a Latin trinomial, but each additionally is given an English name mostly reflecting the colour of the head.

During ornithological history a large number of different sub-species have been recorded in Britain, though some of these are now regarded as mutant versions of our native yellow wagtail rather than vagrants. The yellow wagtail *M.f. flavissima* breeds only in Britain and at a few spots in adjacent France. The blue-headed *M.f. flava* breeds on the adjacent Continent and occasionally in south-east England; it also hybridizes with the yellow wagtail and may then produce young with characteristics of other sub-species. Thus watching yellow wagtails can prove very exciting or very tricky depending on one's viewpoint.

Habitat: Flooded or damp grasslands, usually inland along rivers often with cattle; dry market gardens; coastal marshes; sewage works, reservoirs. Definitely a lowland bird.

Locations: Present over large areas of England, but in Scotland only in the west south of Glasgow; patchy in Wales and more or less absent from Devon and Cornwall. The dry chalk regions of England are unsuited to its needs. On passage frequents marshes and floods in numbers. Unusual sub-species occur mostly in south-east England.

Grey Wagtail *Motacilla cinerea*

Resident: The largest, longest-tailed, and arguably the most attractive of British wagtails, the grey wagtail frequents fast-flowing streams and brooks wherever they can be found. The male is a splendid yellow below and grey above with a bold black bib and prominent white outer tail feathers. Females and juveniles are similar, but the yellow is confined to the belly and undertail. The correlation of British distribution with that of the dipper is high, but the present species is found both further south and east than that stream-side bird.

Habitat: Fast-running streams, also outflows from 'still' waters, weirs, mill races, etc.

Locations: Absent only from east and east-central England, parts of Kent and from Shetland, Orkney and much of the Outer Hebrides. Winters in areas where it does not breed, but such birds are probably of British origin.

Pied Wagtail *Motacilla alba*

Resident: The most common and widespread of British wagtails and, as a result, the bearer of a wealth of affectionate local names. This boldly marked black and white bird frequents waterside habitats, but seems most at home at mill races and weirs even in heavily built up areas. Indeed, in recent years it has occupied a range of urban or industrial habitats and is now found well away from water in many parts of the country. Its habit of roosting communally in large numbers has been observed in areas as diverse as among trees in city centres and inside large greenhouses in market gardens.

Habitat: Very varied; typically beside water but extends to urban and industrial sites as well as totally dry locations.

Locations: Virtually absent from Shetland, otherwise found in every part of Britain.

Passage Migrant: There is a regular passage of the Continental white wagtail *M.a. alba* which has a grey not black back and is, therefore, easily recognised in the field. In autumn young pied wagtails also have grey backs and care must be taken in making a positive sub-specific identification. In spring there is no problem and these birds may be quite widespread in many parts of the country.

Locations: Any coastal area, but also inland.

Waxwing *Bombycilla garrulus*

Winter Visitor: Waxwings are regular winter visitors in variable numbers to the northern parts of the east coast of Britain. They are typical birds of the northern taiga zone and have a wide distribution in the sub-Arctic save in eastern North America where they are replaced by the very similar cedar waxwing. They feed mainly on berries and regularly migrate southwards in their search for food. However, about every three or four years a population explosion creates the right conditions for an eruption and then huge numbers of birds descend on the southern forests and spill over into the more temperate regions of Europe including Britain. This may be triggered off by a food shortage, but the results can be quite spectacular in Britain. There is evidence of onward movement, though most birds seem to winter, and of a spring return. Irruptions are seldom noted before October and birds return during March.

Habitat: Northern coniferous forests; in Britain along hedgerows, in gardens, and anywhere else with a good berry crop.

Locations: Shetland, north Norfolk and in between every year; elsewhere in major irruption years.

Dipper *Cinclus cinclus*

Resident: A large, chunky, unmistakable bird with a specialized ecological niche that prevents its appearance and residence anywhere but on fast-flowing hill streams. The dipper bears a strong physical resemblance to the wren, but is several times the size of that bird, has a white blaze across the chest, and feeds on or below the water's surface. Each pair defends a territory that may be up to two miles in length, but only a few yards across. It is best searched for by stopping at bridges over suitable streams and peering upstream and downstream. Boulders in such streams are invariably marked white with droppings.
Habitat: Fast flowing streams.
Locations: Confined to the hilly districts of Britain and absent east of a line drawn from Swanage to Bempton, from western Cornwall, the Isle of Man, much of Lancashire and Cheshire, parts of lowland Scotland, much of the Outer Hebrides and Orkneys, and from Shetland.
Winter Visitor: A few Continental birds (called black-bellied dippers) occur on the east coast and along streams in southern England in winter, as do our own birds that wander from their native streams.
Locations: None specific.

Wren *Troglodytes troglodytes*

Resident: The sole Old World representative of an extremely numerous New World family whose members range in size up to that of the jay. The wren (called 'winter wren' in North America) is a remarkably successful species that has occupied every corner of Britain and is abundant in virtually every habitat. It may number as many as seven million pairs, although it is hard hit by severe winters as a result of which numbers may be less than a quarter of this figure. Although Continental birds arrive in autumn to winter with us, British wrens are notoriously tenacious in maintaining their residence here. As a result several quite discrete populations have evolved, some of which merit

sub-specific status. Thus we have the St Kilda wren, Shetland wren, Fair Isle wren and so on.
Habitat: From urban backyards, through gardens, farmland and woods to moorland, cliffs, mountain gullies and isolated islands and stacks.
Locations: Everywhere throughout Britain.

Dunnock *Prunella modularis*

Resident: Accentors, for it is to the Prunellidae or family of accentors that the dunnock belongs, are with a single exception birds of the highest mountains – the exception is the dunnock itself. Yet the dunnock, or 'hedge accentor' as it used to be more acceptably called, is actually absent in Britain only from the highest of the high hills. In typical accentor fashion it creeps along the ground, skulks in the bottoms of hedges, and sings its attractive jingling little song atop a bush.
Habitat: Scrub, parkland, gardens, felled woodland, hedgerows.
Locations: Found everywhere throughout Britain save for the Grampian-Cairngorm massif, some of the hills north of the Caledonian Canal, parts of the Outer Hebrides and Shetland. Elsewhere it is widespread with approaching four million pairs in the country as a whole.

Robin *Erithacus rubecula*

Resident: The robin is Britain's national bird as well as one of the best known and most loved. While in many parts of Europe it is a skulking woodland bird, in this country it has become tame and now seems most at home in suburban gardens. The total population is not much short of four million pairs and the species' well-known lack of tolerance of its fellows ensures that these are well spread out through the length and breadth of the land. Strangely enough its distribution bears a remarkable similarity to that of the dunnock.
Habitat: Gardens, parks, woodland, hedgerows.
Locations: Throughout Britain save for the Cairngorm-Grampians, parts of Caithness and the Outer Hebrides, and Shetland. Elsewhere widespread and numerous.

Winter Visitor: Continental migrants arrive on the east coast in October and set all the resident birds calling and displaying. Some pass on further south.

Locations: None specific.

Nightingale *Luscinia megarhynchos*

Summer Visitor: Though such an outstanding songster and a bird that has found its way into the folklore and literature of Britain, the nightingale is seldom seen either on spring or autumn passage. It does not arrive in any numbers until the end of April, sings in May and June, and is away by August. As a result the opportunities for seeing it are quite definitely restricted to a few, altogether too brief, weeks. It breeds right across Europe from Spain and France to Turkey and beyond into Asia. Yet Britain is right on the edge of its range. Numbers have shown a disastrous decline in recent years, probably due to drought conditions in its winter quarters in the Sahel zone of Africa.

Habitat: Heaths with blackthorn; coppiced woodland with standards.

Locations: To look north of Yorkshire or west of Dorset for this bird is virtually pointless; barely a handful nest north or west of a line drawn from the Severn to the Humber. It is most numerous in south-east England in the Weald where coppices of five to eight years of age can be found.

Bluethroat *Luscinia svecica*

Passage Migrant: This attractive, though usually secretive, little chat is essentially a ground bird that seldom ventures very far from cover. In the breeding season it is marked by a bright blue throat, though in winter and in juvenile plumage this is less obvious or even absent altogether. At all times a bright rust-red tail pattern is the surest means of identification. The bluethroat breeds from France right across Eurasia to Alaska, but is absent as a breeding bird from Britain. A female was discovered on eggs in Scotland in 1968, but they were taken by a predator. It is thus no more than a scarce migrant to our shores, almost always in autumn, though a few occur in spring.

Habitat: Dwarf vegetation, bushy scrub; on passage almost entirely coastal.

Locations: An east coast species that can be looked for from August through to October from Shetland to Kent, but with a preponderance of records from the well-watched localities – Fair Isle, Spurn, Cley.

Black Redstart *Phoenicurus ochruros*

Summer Visitor: The black redstart colonized Britain during the years between the two wars, but only really became established after the Second World War on the bombed sites of central London. Gradually it has moved out and spread to other sites and to other parts of the country, although the population is still less than a hundred pairs. Throughout this lengthy period it has remained mostly an urban bird, though some of the earliest colonists nested on cliffs and there is now a tendency to do so again. Nevertheless old and dirty railway yards, power stations and industrial sites remain favoured haunts.

Habitat: Industrial and urban wasteland, sea cliffs.

Locations: Nests at Flamborough Head and Beachy Head, and along the coast at various points between; in London and its surrounds; and at scattered spots in the west Midlands.

Redstart *Phoenicurus phoenicurus*

Summer Visitor: Like several other species that winter in the Sahel, the redstart has suffered a considerable decline in numbers in recent years doubtless stemming from the drought that has so affected life in that part of Africa. As a result it has abandoned considerable areas of Britain where once it was quite numerous – notably East Anglia. It is present from late April to the end of September.

Habitat: Woodland edges, heaths and hedgerows with old trees, parkland; also nests in nest boxes and holes in walls.

Locations: Most numerous in the west particularly in the hanging oak woods of Wales and in other damp woodland with a plentiful supply of holes. Absent from Shetland, Orkney and Outer Hebrides, Caithness, north-east Aberdeenshire and large areas of Lincolnshire and East Anglia, also from south-west Cornwall.

Passage Migrant: A common passage migrant on the east coast in autumn until October and even November. At such times it invariably accompanies pied flycatchers and other 'typical' Scandinavian species. *Locations:* Whole of the east coast from Shetland to Kent.

Whinchat *Saxicola rubetra*

Summer Visitor: Whinchats arrive in Britain throughout April, though the bulk of birds do not arrive until May. Autumn passage may continue into October, but most birds have departed by the end of September. Between times they can be found in a variety of open landscapes where, characteristically, they will sit atop some low perch. This may consist of a post, barbed-wire fence, low bush, or particularly a young conifer, for it is in plantations at an early stage of their growth that whinchats find their ideal habitat. However, any area of rough ground with perches will suffice. Identification poses few problems for only the stonechat is at all similar but in all plumages it lacks the creamy-white eyebrow of the whinchat.
Habitat: Rough ground with low perches; heaths, hillsides, young plantations.
Locations: Its need of rough ground restricts the whinchat to the more westerly and northern regions of Britain and it is particularly abundant among the Welsh hills, in the Pennines and southern Scotland. It avoids the mountain tops and is absent from Shetland. In lowland England it is absent from large areas of Lincolnshire, Norfolk and Suffolk, but is quite numerous where heathland is available as, for instance, in the Brecks and New Forest. It is widespread on passage and may then occur virtually anywhere.

Stonechat *Saxicola torquata*

Resident: Though similar to the whinchat, this delightful little bird is easily identified by the black (or dark) head, a white half collar and the lack of a white eye-brow. It perches even more obviously than that species atop a bush (often gorse), but also on posts and telegraph wires and is generally tame and approachable. Though it breeds inland over large areas of its huge range, which extends right across Asia and

Africa, in Britain it is mainly a coastal bird save in the south-west and in western Scotland. Whereas the whinchat prefers grassy areas, the stonechat has a quite definite penchant for heather. Both are commonly found in young conifer plantations, but the ground cover determines which species will occupy an individual planting. Though it can be found throughout the year there is some emigration and internal movements take birds to areas where they do not breed.

Habitat: Mainly coastal commons and heaths with gorse and heather, but also young conifer plantations.

Locations: Inland in England the stonechat is found on the Surrey heaths and on Dartmoor; elsewhere it is mainly coastal, from Sussex westwards and along Welsh and Scottish coasts northwards to the Firth of Forth. On the east coast it is much less widely distributed, though the Suffolk heaths and east Kent still have some pairs. It is absent from Shetland.

Wheatear *Oenanthe oenanthe*

Summer Visitor: Generally one of the earliest of summer visitors to arrive, the wheatear is a welcome sign of spring as from mid-March. There are, however, records as early as the beginning of February and as late as the end of December. Unfortunately wheatears have declined drastically over the past few decades, especially in southern England. Reasons for its disappearance from many previous haunts are not difficult to find, but changing agricultural techniques is by far the most important one. Ploughing marginal land, the abandonment of sheep grazing, the introduction of myxamatosis and the subsequent decline of the rabbit – all had an effect on the short-grass areas needed by wheatears. Elsewhere in the hill country of the north and west the wheatear remains a familiar bird.

Habitat: Short-grass areas; hills and moors, but also shingle spits and other coastal areas.

Locations: Throughout the hills of Wales, the Pennines, the Lake District and Scotland the wheatear is a common sight. Elsewhere it tends to be coastal save in the Brecks, the New Forest, Dartmoor and Exmoor. Most coasts have a scattering of birds save for much of Yorkshire and Lincolnshire. On passage wheatears can turn up virtually anywhere that suitable habitat exists.

Ring Ouzel *Turdus torquatus*

Summer Visitor: This close relative of the blackbird replaces that species among the hills and mountains of northern and western Britain. It is nowhere very common and the total British population of about 15,000 pairs means that it is never really obvious even on migration. For most bird-watchers this remains one of the species that requires a visit to the hills. It is readily separated from the blackbird by the bold white crescent on the breast and, in less favourable views, by the silver sheen on the wing in flight. It is generally present from late March through to October and, though some individuals occasionally winter, this habit is far less prevalent than it was last century.

Habitat: Moorland and hills with rocky outcrops or screes, and deep gullies, often with dwarf bushes.

Locations: A drastic decline in numbers during the present century, though still present in most areas over 1,000 feet. Scottish Highlands, Border Hills, Lake District, Pennines, Yorkshire Moors, Welsh hills and Dartmoor and Exmoor all have ring ouzels breeding. On passage it may turn up virtually anywhere in open country, though it is never numerous.

Blackbird *Turdus merula*

Resident: Somewhere between five and six million pairs of blackbirds breed in Britain, making the species one of the most numerous as well as one of the most widespread of British birds. Its catholic choice of habitat, which covers virtually every landform save for the highest hills, has enabled it to spread throughout the country while the gradual improvement in the British climate has facilitated its spread northwards to the Shetlands this century. As a result it is among the most familiar of all British birds. Late autumn sees a considerable immigration of Continental blackbirds particularly to the east coast, some of which pass onwards to France others augment our native birds.

Habitat: Virtually ubiquitous; absent only from highest hills.

Locations: Everywhere save for Grampian–Cairngorm massif and some of the highest hills north of the Great Glen.

Fieldfare *Turdus pilaris*

Resident: The fieldfare's claim to British residence rests on the fact that it has bred here every year since 1967. Though only a handful of pairs do so today they are nevertheless spread from Shetland (regular) south to the Peak District.
Habitat: Woodland and scrub, forestry plantations and farmland, but invariably in hilly districts. Nest usually close to water.
Locations: Too scarce a bird to offer exact locations, nesting fieldfares may be sought in Shetland, Orkney, the eastern Scottish Highlands, and the Pennines south to Derbyshire.
Winter Visitor: In contrast truly huge numbers of fieldfares arrive in Britain from September and stay through to April. They form nomadic flocks, often in company with redwings, and range over hedgerows and damp grassy fields and meadows in their search for food. There is a quite definite return movement starting in the south of the country in March.
Locations: Throughout the country.

Song Thrush *Turdus philomelos*

Resident: Though nowhere as numerous as the blackbird, this species too has proved remarkably successful in adapting to the man-made landscape of Britain. It is found virtually throughout the country, and is as at home in a town garden as it is in a mountain glen. Its familiar spotted breast is confusable only with the redwing and the mistle thrush, but these are both distinct birds in their different ways. In winter our resident song thrush population is joined by migrants from the Continent.
Habitat: Short-grass or bare woodland floors; also hedgerows, orchards, gardens and parks, and heaths.
Locations: Absent only from the high Scottish hills, from parts of Lewis and from Shetland.

Redwing *Turdus iliacus*

Resident: Only a few years ago about 200–300 pairs of redwings bred annually in Scotland. Though regular breeding was established as recently as 1967, there have been intermittent reports from as long ago as 1925. This clear and successful colonization was doubtless attributable to the climatic changes that have also brought several other Scandinavian species to our shores to breed. However, recent years have seen a serious decline with numbers down to two figures.

Habitat: A wide variety of niches have been utilized including gardens, hillside woods and woodland edges; but most are adjacent to water.

Locations: Scottish Highlands with most nests north of the Great Glen or on Speyside. Wester Ross has the highest population.

Winter Visitor: Large numbers of redwings winter in Britain arriving in October and departing again in April. They form nomadic flocks often mixing with fieldfares and feeding along hedgerows and particularly on splashy grassland.

Locations: Throughout the country.

Mistle Thrush *Turdus viscivorus*

Resident: Though it is equally as widespread, the mistle thrush is much thinner on the ground than its smaller relative, the song thrush. It has larger territories and may be outnumbered by as many as five to one. Nevertheless it occupies a wide range of habitats and has been just as successful in moving into city parks as the song thrush. It is an early breeder and usually has eggs before the trees are fully leaved. For this reason it frequently builds a nest in the crotch of a tree, and it is this same early breeding that leads it to establish a territory during the latter part of the winter and merit the country name of 'storm cock'. It is larger and greyer than a song thrush and has white tips to the corners of its tail.

Habitat: Open country with trees, heaths, hedgerows, parks, gardens; also moorland.

Locations: A widespread species that is absent only from the high Scottish hills, from much of Caithness, from several of the Inner Hebrides, from the Outer Hebrides except Stornoway Woods, and completely from Orkney and Shetland.

Cetti's Warbler *Cettia cetti*

Resident: The first record of Cetti's warbler in Britain was in 1961 and the species remained a very rare vagrant until the end of that decade. In the early 1970s it began to breed in Kent and since then has exploded in numbers and range so that an estimated 150 pairs now breed over most southern coastal counties between Cornwall and Norfolk. Though it is an undistinguished 'little brown job' with a rounded tail its extraordinary explosive song is instantly recognizable. Its colonization of Britain follows a spread northwards across Europe that is almost as spectacular as that of the collared dove.

Habitat: Tangled bushes usually near water, often at the edges of marshes.

Locations: Though present at over forty locations along the south and east coasts, only Stodmarsh can be named as a definite spot. Fortunately this area of the Stour Valley is also the species' British headquarters. Generally best observed in spring while singing – very elusive at other times.

Grasshopper Warbler *Locustella naevia*

Summer Visitor: Generally present from late April to September the grasshopper warbler was, until quite recently, the only 'reeler' present in Britain. However, colonization by small numbers of Savi's warblers over the past few years has introduced an element of possible confusion when attempts are made to identify a 'reeling' call from a reed bed. Grasshopper warblers are, however, far more catholic in their choice of habitat than are Savi's and, though both may be found in reed beds, the present species is also present in young plantations, in downland scrub and on heaths. It is also a 'streaked' rather than 'plain' brown warbler with a noticeable eyebrow.

Habitat: Reeded margins, marshes, heaths, tangled vegetation on downs, young conifer plantations.

Locations: Present throughout the country, but becoming progressively thinner on the ground the further north and the higher one goes. Absent from Shetland and most of Orkney and the Outer Hebrides. Decidedly scarce in the Highlands and the Pennines. Good spots include all the east coast bird haunts – Holme, Cley, Walberswick, Hickling, Minsmere.

Savi's Warbler *Locustella luscinioides*

Summer Visitor: Savi's warblers bred among the Fens during the middle part of the last century and were then absent until they colonized Kent in 1960. This colony has now expanded, birds have spread to several other parts of the country and a population of over 20 singing males has become established. The species is a true 'marshland' warbler and its habitat is always very wet, its favorite one being large reed beds with sedges. Like the grasshopper warbler it has a 'reeling' song, but its uniform brown colouring is quite different and it is much less catholic in its choice of habitat. The actual reeling, moreover, is pitched lower and is quite distinct from that of the grasshopper warbler once learned. Singing starts soon after the birds arrive in mid-April.

Habitat: Reed beds without or without sedges and bushes, also sedges without reeds, but always very damp.

Locations: Savi's warblers can be found in Devon (2 sites); Dorset (1); Hampshire (1); Kent at Stodmarsh, the site of the original colonization; Norfolk (2); Suffolk at Minsmere and Walberswick; Warwick (1); Humberside (1); and Stafford (1).

Sedge Warbler
Acrocephalus schoenobaenus

Summer Visitor: Present from late April through to September, the sedge warbler is one of the most typical of wetland birds and also one of the most numerous. Its strange grating calls can be confused with those of both reed and marsh warblers as they issue from deep within a reed bed, but they are characteristic once learned. In habitat it is more catholic than either, being found away from reed beds and sedges with great regularity and being prepared to colonize virtually any waterside or damp vegetation. The song flight which is performed from arrival till early July is delightful and diagnostic.

Habitat: Reed beds, often with sallows or alders; rank waterside scrub; even away from water in young conifer plantations.

Locations: Characteristic of the larger wetland areas of south and east England, the sedge warbler is much thinner on the ground in both north and west, but particularly where hilly districts preclude the creation of the wetlands it prefers. Absent from Shetland, the Highlands, Pennines, Welsh Hills and Dartmoor, otherwise widely distributed. Good numbers in the major reed bed reserves such as Leighton Moss, Fairburn Ings, Cley, Hickling, Horsey, Walberswick, Minsmere, Stodmarsh, Radipole etc.

Top The cliffs of the north and west of Britain hold spectacular colonies of seabirds that are among the most important of our ornithological heritages. These **guillemots**, with **kittiwakes** below, were photographed in Shetland.

Bottom The **kestrel** is the most familiar of our birds of prey and can be frequently seen hovering over open areas including the margins of motorways.

A male **hawfinch** feeds his mate as part of courtship. This is an exceptionally difficult bird to locate, though it is both widespread and not uncommon.

Marsh Warbler *Acrocephalus palustris*

Summer Visitor: One of the latest of summer visitors to reach our shores, the marsh warbler is seldom present before late May and normally arrives only in early June. By the end of August most have departed. It is also a very scarce bird and one that has, on occasion in the past, caused a great deal of confusion particularly with reed warblers. The species are, in fact, so similar that they are best separated by song. Even here, however, all is far from simple. The marsh warbler is frequently regarded as one of the best of British songsters, but it also sings gratingly like a reed warbler and is an accomplished mimic to boot. With a total population of less than a hundred pairs this is far from being an easy bird to see.

Habitat: Drier areas than the reed warbler, but invariably close to water. Nettles and meadowsweet with some bushes are the typical nesting site, though osier beds were formerly much favoured.

Locations: The vast majority of marsh warblers nest in the Severn and Avon Valleys in Worcestershire with Tewkesbury being the acknowledged centre. Elsewhere in southern England they nest in Kent and Surrey, Dorset and Somerset, but numbers are few. On passage they are virtually non-existent. Crucial to search in the last week of May and first two weeks of June while the birds are in song.

Reed Warbler *Acrocephalus scirpaceus*

Summer Visitor: A later arrival than the sedge warbler with large numbers seldom present before May. By late September the majority have departed. To the beginner the reed warbler presents an identification problem of major proportions – it is brown above, creamy below and totally lacking in any features that might help put a name to it. It is, however, this very lack of features that eliminates most other birds save for the very similar marsh and Savi's warblers, and a few extreme rarities. More than any other warbler it is aptly named, for it is seldom found far from the common reed. It may nest in hawthorn, meadowsweet etc., but reeds are always nearby.

Habitat: Reed beds with or without other vegetation.

Locations: Reed warblers are confined to south and east England and are all but absent from Scotland and most of Wales. A line drawn from the Humber to the Ribble and thence directly south to Lyme Regis encloses almost all of their UK range. To the north they breed as far as Leighton Moss, and to the west they do so as far as Oxwich Bay in Wales and Marazion in Cornwall. Over the rest of England they are numerous wherever large reed beds can be found.

Icterine Warbler *Hippolais icterina*

Vagrant: A large, yellow-green, slightly ungainly warbler, with a dagger-like bill accentuated by a shallow-sloping forehead, this bird occurs irregularly in spring and autumn. It is one of a pair of species, the other being the melodious warbler, that between them occupy the Continent. The present species is the easterly one with a range that extends from northern and eastern France to southern Scandinavia and through eastern Europe to Russia beyond the Urals. Both species are olive above and yellow below and require great care to distinguish – the present species has a longer wing marked by a pale wing panel. It is occasionally identified in spring in May or June, but is more numerous in autumn.

Habitat: Woodland edges, parks, gardens; in Britain virtually any vegetation available.

Locations: In spring more or less confined to Fair Isle. In autumn found at bird observatories and other 'hot spots' on the east and south coasts; Fair Isle, Shetland, Spurn, Gibraltar Point, Holme, Blakeney, Holkham, Cley, Sandwich Bay, Dungeness, Portland, Isles of Scilly. But this distribution must represent a strong observer bias. Last week of August and first week of September is the peak period.

Melodious Warbler *Hippolais polyglotta*

Vagrant: A species pair with the icterine warbler, the melodius occupies a westerly range that includes Iberia, most of France, and Italy. It is a green-yellow warbler with a more rounded wing than the icterine, but which like the latter is primarily an autumn vagrant to our shores. It is most likely to occur at the end of August or during the first three weeks of September, but with perhaps a more westerly bias than the icterine.

Habitat: Woodland edges, parks, gardens, groves.
Locations: Virtually unknown in spring. In autumn occurs at southern and western bird observatories and coastal 'hot spots', Isles of Scilly, Skokholm, Bardsey, Portland – but with less of a bias than was previously thought. It may thus also turn up on the east coast from time to time.

Dartford Warbler *Sylvia undata*

Resident: Apart from the recently colonizing Cetti's warbler, the Dartford is Britain's only resident warbler. It is also right on the northern fringe of its range and, as a result, is particularly prone to population fluctuations mostly as a result of hard weather. During severe winters bird-watchers are always conscious of the fact that the species could easily be lost, but although only handfuls of pairs survive they soon return to their former numbers. It is, however, doubtful if its population ever reaches more than a thousand pairs. Loss of habitat progressively restricts the speed of recolonization as suitable heaths tend to become ever more isolated.
Habitat: Heaths with heather and dense gorse.
Locations: Best looked for during the breeding season when singing facilitates observation of what is a very secretive little bird. Locations are difficult to list, but the species is more or less confined to the Surrey, Sussex, New Forest and Dorset heaths. Only at Arne are Dartford warblers available to view.

Barred Warbler *Sylvia nisoria*

Passage Migrant: Sufficient numbers of barred warblers occur in Britain each year to avoid the species being classified as a 'vagrant'. However, it is always scarce and even keen bird-watchers may miss it for a year or so. The species is a 'chunky' *Sylvia* warbler which, in the adult, is boldly barred on the chest and flanks. Immatures lack this barring and it is these rather nondescript birds that occur in Britain every autumn. They are best identified by a distinct wing bar and white tips to the inner flight feathers. Spring records are exceptional.

Habitat: Woodland edges particularly with thorns, hedgerows; on passage virtually any vegetation available.

Locations: From August to about mid-October from Shetland to Suffolk on the east coast. Cley and Holkham always get more than their fair share, but other spots do well enough – Fair Isle, Isle of May.

Lesser Whitethroat *Sylvia curruca*

Summer Visitor: A widespread Old World species that finds Britain right at the edge of its range and which is, like so many other such species, more common in the south and the east. However, it does not migrate southwards to winter in the Sahel as does the whitethroat and, as a result, did not suffer the disastrous slump in numbers that afflicted that species at the end of the 1960s due to the severe drought in Africa. In some areas it may now be the more common of the two species. Like the other *Sylvia* warblers it is far from keen to show itself and its presence is best detected by its rattling song and harsh call note. When viewed its grey (not rufous) back and distinctly 'spectacled' look are diagnostic.

Habitat: Open woodland and scrub with dense ground cover, usually in areas with thicker cover than the whitethroat.

Locations: A bird of south and east England that is scarce in the south-west beyond the Exe; in Wales beyond the border country; and in the north beyond the Lake District to the west and Lindisfarne to the east. It is also absent from the Pennines. Best looked for in May, but present until September.

Whitethroat *Sylvia communis*

Summer Visitor: Formerly one of the most abundant of summer visitors to Britain, the fearful drought that afflicted the Sahel zone immediately south of the Sahara from 1969 onwards decimated the numbers of this species, thus showing that winter quarters are as important as breeding zones to migratory birds. A decline from about five million to less than one million pairs is a fair estimate. Even so the whitethroat remains widespread, and not uncommon in Britain. It is present from late April to September and is most easily seen in May or June, when its characteristic song flight and parachute descent to a high bush or similar perch are a familiar sight. The chattering song may also be uttered from deep cover.

Habitat: Scrub, plantations, woodland edges, rough ground, hedgerows.

Locations: Present throughout Britain and absent only from parts of the Pennines, the highest Welsh hills, the Border hills and much of the Highlands and northern Scotland. The Outer Hebrides have it at Stornoway Woods, but in Orkney and Shetland it is absent.

Garden Warbler *Sylvia borin*

Summer Visitor: Arrives in late April and early May and stays through to September. The garden warbler is a strangely nondescript little bird that, lacking any noticeable features, can easily be mistaken for a number of quite different species of quite disparate genera. Thus it is an easy bird to turn into a rare *Hippolais* warbler, but may also be confused with an *Acrocephalus*. Indeed it is *the* be-careful warbler of Europe. In spring its song is both diagnostic and a delight – it warbles on in a subdued sort of way very like a blackcap, but lacking the higher pitched notes of that excellent songster.

Habitat: Woods with good covering of undergrowth of moderate height, but also in scrubland and young plantations.

Locations: Present over most of England and Wales with notable absences in the Fens and Lancashire. Becoming thinner on the ground in Scotland, decidedly scarce in the Highlands, and absent from Orkney, Shetland and most of the Inner and Outer Hebrides.

Blackcap *Sylvia atricapilla*

Summer Visitor: One of the very few warblers that winters in small numbers in south and south-west England, and one that returns early to bring a breath of spring to the country before the end of March. However, most blackcaps do not arrive until well into April and then their delicious song vies with that of the nightingale for the title of best

British songster. The sweet warbling is broken by virtuoso passages that delight the ear. This all-grey bird is marked by a black cap in the male – beware confusion with marsh and willow tits – and a gingery cap in the female.

Habitat: Woodland, deciduous or mixed, with strong shrub layer; hedgerows, plantations, scrub.

Locations: A remarkably similar distribution to that of the garden warbler with which it shares much habitat. Becomes thinner on the ground from the Lake District northwards and decidedly scarce in the Highlands. Absent from the Fens, and from Shetland, Orkney and much of the Hebrides. Quite a common bird of passage.

Wood Warbler *Phylloscopus sibilatrix*

Summer Visitor: A very attractive little warbler that is as easy to identify as any other member of this highly confusing and totally fascinating genus. Its bold green upperparts, yellow breast and white belly are much more vividly coloured than any other member of the genus that occurs in Europe, and its bright eyebrow is an additional feature. Its preference for deciduous woods with little or no undergrowth restricts it to mature oak and beech woods over large parts of the country, though in the west (particularly Wales) it is abundant. Its beautiful whirring song uttered in a fluttering display flight beneath the canopy is unique.

Habitat: Mature deciduous woods with scant undergrowth – oaks, beech and, in Scotland, birches.

Locations: Welsh oak woods, Dartmoor valleys, New Forest, Chilterns, North and South Downs, north Norfolk, western Scotland. Absent from much of eastern England, eastern Scotland, the Outer Hebrides, Orkney and Shetland. On passage decidedly scarce.

Chiffchaff *Phylloscopus collybita*

Summer Visitor: Though small numbers of chiffchaffs regularly risk the winter in southern England, the species remains predominantly a summer visitor to most of Britain. The willow warbler, with which it is so easily confused, is about ten times as numerous and much more catholic in its choice of habitat. Though so similar, the songs of the two could not be more distinct, the repeated 'chiff-chaff-chiff-chaff' of the present species contrasting with the melodic descending trill of the willow warbler. On passage great care needs to be take in separating the two by leg colour and by prominence of eyebrow, etc.; they are often lumped together as 'willowchiffs'.

Habitat: Old deciduous and mixed woods with strong undergrowth, plantations, heaths, hedgerows, but with more tall trees than required by willow warbler.

Locations: Apart from the Fens, present throughout southern England. Absent from Pennines, Border hills, and much of Scotland; also from Shetland, Orkney and outer Hebrides save for Stornoway Woods. Spring passage notable, but lack of singing disguises strength of autumn passage.

Willow Warbler *Phylloscopus trochilus*

Summer Visitor: One of the most numerous of British birds and particularly of summer visitors. This attractive little leaf warbler, with its delightful, descending trill of a song, is found throughout Britain often in quite staggering numbers. It is also abundant in Scandinavia and adjacent parts of Continental Europe and, as a result, is a common passage migrant particularly in autumn. It is thus the standard *Phylloscopus* warbler against which all others are compared in the endless search for the extreme rarities that grace our coasts in the late autumn. An eastern brown form may be particularly puzzling at times.

Habitat: Open woodland, but seldom with a definite canopy; birch and Scots pine woods, also scrubby commons and heaths; areas with small bushes or trees including young plantations.

Locations: Save for the Fens and Shetlands the species is present throughout Britain. May be particularly abundant during autumn passage.

Goldcrest *Regulus regulus*

Resident: Britain's tiniest bird and one that is particularly prone to hard winters when its population may be decimated. At times there may be more than a million pairs in the country, at others less than a tenth of that number. Though it is usually associated with coniferous forests, when the population really takes off it may move into deciduous forests in numbers. In appearance it is very similar to the leaf warblers of the genus *Phylloscopus*, of which several species, rare in Britain, may be mistaken for goldcrests. Its high-pitched call notes usually draw attention to it high in some tree where small parties often associate with coal tits. The firecrest, which is its nearest relative, is in fact quite distinct in both appearance and voice.

Habitat: Coniferous forests, but deciduous woods in times of high population.

Locations: With the exception of the Fens, this species is widespread throughout Britain save for Orkney, Shetland and the Outer Hebrides where it is rare.

Firecrest *Regulus ignicapillus*

Resident: The status of this species in Britain is difficult to ascertain exactly. Since 1962 a small, but growing, population has nested in England. Previously the species was known as a regular autumn migrant in small numbers and a rare winter visitor to the south-west. Whether or not the British breeding birds now winter in this country remains obscure, though we can say that firecrests are now present in the country throughout the year. Breeding firecrests may be looked for in Norwegian spruce, but also in many other coniferous and deciduous woods, in May and early June when their 'zit-zit-zit' song can be heard. The striped face pattern serves readily to distinguish them from goldcrests. On passage they occur most regularly on the south coast, but also in East Anglia.

Habitat: Norwegian spruce and other forests.

Locations: The New Forest is the site of their original colonization, but birds have since spread northwards and eastwards and may now be looked for in any suitable woodland. A thorough investigation of a single Buckinghamshire wood produced no less than half the British breeding population. There can be little doubt that this bird is still overlooked in many areas.

Spotted Flycatcher *Muscicapa striata*

Summer Visitor: Arriving in early May and staying on till September the spotted flycatcher is one of the more widespread of our summer visitors. Rather drab and unexciting in appearance, its characteristic method of catching its prey in mid-air, often with an audible snap of its bill, and returning to the same perch to watch out for more passing insects, is a source of great charm. In addition it has the confiding nature of a robin and regularly nests in gardens in specially erected boxes, or among creepers on buildings.

Habitat: Woodland edges or glades, copses, hedgerows, gardens, parks.

Locations: Absent only from the Fens, a few Welsh hills, parts of highest Scotland, the Outer Hebrides (except for Stornoway Woods), Orkney and Shetland.

Pied Flycatcher *Ficedula hypoleuca*

Summer Visitor: This is one of the most attractive and interesting of British birds and one that appeals to bird-watchers in a variety of different ways. As a breeding bird it is confined to deciduous woods in upland valleys reaching its greatest density among the sessile oak woods of Wales. Even here, however, its numbers can be increased and its range expanded by the erection of suitable nest boxes, showing that what British woods need is more holes. As a bird of passage it appeals to a quite different group of bird-watchers. Along the east coast an arrival of pied flycatchers is usually regarded as a key in identifying a 'fall' of Scandinavian birds among which bluethroats may be found. The male's bold black and white plumage can be confused with that of no other regular British bird, while the female and immature resemble the spotted flycatcher, but have no chest streaking and a goodly amount of white in the wing.

Habitat: Deciduous woodland in upland valleys, usually associated with water.

Locations: Devon, Wales, Pennines, Lake District, Yorkshire Moors, the Border country expanding northwards into Scotland, but becoming very thin on the ground in the Highlands. Absent from most of the Hebrides, Orkney and Shetland. In southern and eastern England, save for the north Midlands, is erratic save on passage when it may occur virtually anywhere and can be quite numerous along coasts.

Bearded Tit *Panurus biarmicus*

Resident: Although reduced to only a handful of pairs by the severe winter of 1946–1947 the bearded tit has since recovered, survived another even harsher winter, and spread outwards from its East Anglian strongholds. For long this species was considered a purely Broadland bird, but a huge population build-up in 1959 was followed by eruptive movements that took these birds right across the country to reed beds where they had never been seen before. Further autumn eruptions in subsequent years led to the establishment of breeding colonies as far west as Dorset. Some of these birds even had their origins abroad in Holland. Today bearded tits are as numerous and widespread in England as they have been in historical times.
Habitat: Reed beds, large ones for preference.
Locations: Cley and several north Norfolk reed beds; the Broads, especially Hickling and Horsey; the Suffolk coastal broads such as Walberswick and Minsmere; reed beds along the northern shore of the Blackwater in Essex; Stodmarsh and Sandwich Bay; Pagham; Titchfield; Radipole and the Fleet; and several reed beds in the Humber including Blacktoft Sands. In the autumn bearded tits may now turn up at even quite small reed beds.

Long-tailed Tit *Aegithalos caudatus*

Resident: A widespread species that forms single species flocks that then pass noisily through hedgerows and gardens in their non-stop search for food. Though marked with a fine vinous wash on the underparts, in the field this cannot be seen and the effect is of a dumpy, black and white little bird with a very long tail. It is very rare to encounter a single long-tailed tit and parties of up to about 20 are the norm. Indeed there is even evidence of co-operative breeding with

several adults tending a single nest, and these birds usually roost close together in their search for warmth and protection. Nevertheless severe winters can decimate the numbers of such a small and delicate bird.
Habitat: Hedgerows, scrub, open woodland, commons and heaths with trees.
Locations: Widespread and quite numerous save in areas where climate or habitat are unsuitable, i.e. the Fens, Pennines, some of the Welsh hills, some of the Border hills, much of the Highlands, and the Outer Hebrides, Orkneys and Shetlands. Elsewhere it is not difficult to locate.

Marsh Tit *Parus palustris*

Resident: Marsh and willow tits are so similar in appearance that their respective distributions are still a matter of some confusion due to misidentification, and despite the enormous amount of work that has been devoted to accurately mapping the ranges of British birds. The present species has a glossy cap, a small bib, no pale wing patch and a repeated 'pitcheeoo' call note that is distinctive. Despite its name it is not a marshland bird; indeed there is actually a greater tendency for the willow tit to occur in damp situations where the old and rotten trees that it requires for nesting can be found. For though the marsh tit may peck at the entrance to its nest hole, it does not excavate its own hole in rotten wood as does the willow tit. It often associates with other tits in mixed flocks in woodland, but will also come to bird tables in gardens to feed.
Habitat: Deciduous woods and copses, gardens, commons, but always with trees.
Locations: A widespread species, but one that barely penetrates southern Scotland and is absent from much of the Lake District, western Wales including Anglesey, the Isle of Man, the Fens and London. It is regularly encountered elsewhere and mixed tit flocks in winter usually hold one or two.

Willow Tit *Parus montanus*

Resident: Confusion with what was formerly regarded as the more common marsh tit has precluded the accurate mapping of the willow tit's distribution. It is, however, now regarded as almost as plentiful, with a similar distribution, the only difference being a minor extension into Scotland. The willow tit's high-pitched 'zit-zit-zit' note is far less characteristic than the call of the marsh tit and, for that reason alone, it may frequently be overlooked. The dull, not glossy, cap is not a perfect field mark, but when combined with the larger bib and pale patch in the closed wing, is sufficient under most conditions. The willow tit's predilection for excavating its own nest leads it to occupy damp woods where decaying trees are more plentiful. It has been persuaded to occupy nest boxes by filling them with polystyrene that the bird then removes.

Habitat: Damp woods of alder, willow and birch with rotten stumps or even posts.

Locations: Though found in the Border hills the presence of the willow tit further north in Scotland is highly erratic. It is also absent from much of northern England, North Wales and Anglesey, the Isle of Man, the Fens, London, south Devon and western Cornwall. It is thus slightly more confined than the marsh tit in the south, but extends further in the north. It is likely that the present species has been overlooked and may be more numerous in many areas (on farms for example) than its cogenor.

Crested Tit *Parus cristatus*

Resident: About a thousand pairs of crested tits breed in Britain making it the rarest of British tits and the one with the most restricted range. On the Continent it is found from southern Spain north to Lapland and from Russia to Greece, yet in Britain it is confined to the Scottish Highlands. The reasons for this apparent neglect of Britain are not difficult to find. The species is found only in mature pine forests and is such a tenacious resident that colonization of recent (and older) plantings of these trees would have to be contiguous to its existing breeding range. The alternative of artificial introduction has been debated but not acted upon. Even in the woods where it occurs it is a far from common member of the bird community.

Habitat: Mature pine forests; in Britain is restricted to the last remnants of the Old Caledonian forests plus maturing plantations nearby.

Locations: Confined to the Spey Valley from Rothiemurchus and

Abernethy to the coast at Culbin; to the forests around the Cromarty Firth; and to those in Glen Farrar and Glen Affric. Good spots at Loch Garten and Loch Morlich in Speyside.

Coal Tit *Parus ater*

Resident: Although there is a natural tendency to associate coal tits with conifers, where indeed they are both common and widespread, this association is far from complete. These tiny little birds can also be found in pure deciduous woods such as the oak woods of the Welsh valleys, and the birches of northern Scotland. They often associate with the other common tits to form mixed flocks and in many areas are the most numerous member of such flocks. They frequent higher altitudes than the other species and in such areas will nest in crevices in walls or even on the ground among tree roots. The total population is about three-quarters of a million pairs. The white mark on the nape is a clear identification feature.
Habitat: Coniferous woods, but also deciduous and mixed woods.
Locations: Absent from the Fens, Shetlands, Orkneys, and only sporadic at Stornoway Castle Woods in the Outer Hebrides. Otherwise widespread and easily located.

Blue Tit *Parus caeruleus*

Resident: The most numerous British tit, and one of Britain's most abundant birds. It is arguably the most familiar and best loved of all our birds and certainly has done as much for bird conservation as any species. It comes readily (eagerly!) to bird tables and peanut dispensers, adopts nest boxes as to the manner born, and is a generally tame and pleasant companion to all bird gardeners. Its readiness to nest in boxes has made it an ideal subject of study and intensive work at the Edward Grey Institute at Oxford has led to an understanding of its breeding biology that is second to none and shows interesting pointers to the biology of other species. Blue tits are also found in woods, where they are frequently the dominant species in mixed tit flocks, and in winter they take readily to reed beds.

Habitat: Deciduous, coniferous and mixed woods, heaths and commons, gardens, hedgerows, indeed virtually anywhere with trees.
Locations: Absent from Shetland, Orkney, the Outer Hebrides save for Stornoway Woods, parts of Sutherland and Caithness, the Cairngorm and Grampian massif, Col and Tiree, but otherwise numerous throughout Britain. The bird-seeker generally need look no further than his own peanut dispenser.

Great Tit *Parus major*

Resident: Well in excess of two million pairs of great tits nest regularly with us, making the species one of the most numerous of British birds. It is as familiar in our gardens as the blue tit, though perhaps not as numerous, and in deciduous woodlands sometimes outnumbers the smaller species. It takes food from bird tables and peanut dispensers and is generally more aggressive in its feeding. It will occupy nest boxes and has extended its range northwards with the establishment of plantations in Scotland. The colonization of Stornoway Woods in the Outer Hebrides is very recent.
Habitat: Woods of all types, hedgerows, gardens, heaths, commons, parks.
Locations: Widespread and abundant throughout the country save for the Scottish hills, Orkney, Shetland, the Outer Hebrides except at Stornoway, and a few treeless spots in the Fens.

Nuthatch *Sitta europaea*

Resident: The nuthatch is one of the more successful of Old World birds. Its range extends from Spain right across Europe and Siberia to Japan and the Bering Sea, with a huge southward extension to take in China, Korea, South-east Asia and the sweaty jungles of central India. Throughout this huge area it is totally dependent on trees, which it climbs with consummate ease both upwards and downwards, and without which it cannot exist. Though the name stems accurately from its ability to hack open nuts, that is, nut-hack not nut-hatch, it takes a wide variety of food that it finds among the bark crevices of predominantly deciduous trees. Its shrill whistling call is easily recognised and draws attention to it in the densest of woods. It occasionally takes to nest boxes, but will plaster up the entrance hole with mud even if it is the right size.

Habitat: Deciduous and mixed forests, gardens and even mature hedgerows.

Locations: Widespread in English and Welsh woods and thus absent only from the Fens and the East Anglian prairies, parts of Lincolnshire, Yorkshire and Lancashire and much of the north including the Lake District. In Scotland a couple of records may indicate colonization from abroad.

Treecreeper *Certhia familiaris*

Resident: This delicate little woodland bird is well camouflaged and may easily be overlooked as it works its way circular-fashion up the trunks of trees. At the top of a trunk it simply drops down to the foot of the next and repeats the process onwards throughout the forest. Its thin, decurved bill is ideally suited to probing into bark crevices in its search for insects and their larvae. That such a niche is vacant, despite the presence of nuthatches and woodpeckers, is apparent by the species' success. It enjoys a completely circumpolar distribution across Eurasia and North America (where it is confusingly called the 'brown creeper') with extensions southwards through Mexico and into Central America, and in Asia into the Himalayas. Its nest is well hidden behind loose bark or in a broken or split trunk, but a specifically designed nest box may tempt it on occasion.

Habitat: Deciduous and coniferous woodland in Britain only; on the Continent it is confined to conifers, its niche in deciduous woods being occupied by the closely related short-toed treecreeper.

Locations: Mainland Britain with absences only from the treeless Fens and major hill areas and moors of northern England and Scotland. Absent from Shetland, Orkney and the Outer Hebrides save for Stornoway Woods which it colonized in 1962.

Golden Oriole *Oriolus oriolus*

Summer Visitor: Golden orioles are found in southern England in small numbers regularly every year between late April and June. Their bright black and yellow colours, particularly in the male, would seem to make them a conspicuous species, whereas they are easily overlooked among woodland. Fortunately the loud, melodic flute-like song is both easily recognised and audible over long distances and it is this that draws attention to their presence. A fair proportion of these 'spring' orioles stay on to breed, though it would seem that breeding is often overlooked once singing stops. Though most birds appear as a result of spring overshooting, there is evidence of birds returning to the same breeding site in successive years, and also of a very thin scattering in autumn.

Habitat: Deciduous woodland, occasionally mixed with conifers.

Locations: Best looked for from April through to June in all southern counties of England; Isles of Scilly, Devon, Sussex, Kent, Essex and Suffolk are the best, with records in Scilly as regular as anywhere. Also regular in Gwent.

Red-backed Shrike *Lanius collurio*

Summer Visitor: Once widespread over southern England the red-backed shrike has declined drastically as a breeding bird over the past decade and is now something of a rarity. A total of less than 50 pairs remain. However, the outlook is not all gloom and despondency. In 1970 a pair was present in Orkney, since when other parts of Scotland have been colonized in much the same way as the wryneck has colonized northern Britain while disappearing from the south. Reasons offered for the decline and colonization are many and various and, though there has undoubtedly been a considerable destruction of heathland habitat, climatic change seems by far the most likely cause.

Habitat: Heathland with bushes and trees, downland, gardens.

Locations: In England is confined south of a line drawn between the Severn and The Wash. Dorset and Hampshire, the Brecks, and the Suffolk and Norfolk coastal heaths still have them. In Scotland localities remain unpublishable during the colonizing period. Present from early May to September.

Great Grey Shrike *Lanius excubitor*

Winter Visitor: Great grey shrikes enjoy a huge circumpolar distri-

Lesser spotted woodpecker. Smallest of our woodpeckers and easily overlooked as it feeds among the canopy of woodland and hedgerow.

Top **Arctic terns** are summer visitors to Britain, particularly the north. They hand out rough justice to those who penetrate their breeding colonies and may draw blood from the scalp of an intruder – be warned.
Bottom **Brent geese** of the dark-bellied form. Under strict protection this marine goose has prospered and spread as a winter visitor to our coastal estuaries and shorelines.

bution that takes them right across Eurasia from Spain to the Bering Straits and onwards from coast to coast of North America where they are known as 'northern shrikes'. In the western Palearctic they breed from Morocco north to Lapland yet there is not a single record of breeding in Britain. With us the species remains a scarce winter visitor.

Habitat: Woodland edge, heaths with trees, hedgerows.

Locations: Regular from October to March along the east coast from Shetland to Kent, and at some inland heaths. North Norfolk, east Suffolk and the Surrey heaths usually have winter residents.

Jay *Garrulus glandarius*

Resident: Despite its size, fine colouring and harsh raucous cries the jay is by no means an obvious bird. It frequents woodland and easily disappears among the leaves of the canopy: indeed it is usually seen in laboured flight as it moves from one part of the forest to another. This self-effacing quality is undoubtedly part of the jay's instinctive behaviour pattern, though it could be learned as most hands are turned against it for one reason or another. Though it depends on nuts and berries in winter and has been held responsible for speeding up the post-glacial spread of oak forests by its habit of burying acorns, in summer it is a voracious predator of the eggs and young of other birds.

Habitat: Woodlands, both deciduous and coniferous; also in parks and gardens, even in the centres of large cities.

Locations: Widespread in England and Wales wherever suitable woodland is found. Absent from the Fens and Pennines. In Scotland is found in the southern part of the Border hills, but is then absent northwards up to the southern Highlands. This gap may indicate that the Highland birds are of Scandinavian stock.

Magpie *Pica pica*

Resident: The magpie is a highly successful species that has managed to spread throughout Eurasia from Britain to the Bering Straits, and even to colonize Alaska and a large area of western North America as far south as the Mexican border. Its bold black and white plumage makes it a familiar bird of the British countryside, though its depredations on young gamebirds make it a prime target of gamekeepers. In recent years it has spread into suburbs and heavily built-up areas and has even taken to raiding bird tables for food.

Habitat: Woodland edges, hedgerows, copses and dells, parks and gardens.

Locations: Absent only from the Fens and East Anglian prairies, from much of the Border hills and northern Pennines, and from the Highlands, Hebrides, Orkney and Shetland. Otherwise widespread and numerous.

Chough *Pyrrhocorax pyrrhocorax*

Resident: Although a mountain bird over most of its range, which extends from Spain to China, in Britain choughs are confined to sea cliffs save for the population of North Wales which is now found in disused slate quarries. Over the past hundred years there has been a serious decline in numbers, perhaps associated with an increase in the number of hard winters, and the chough is now one of our rarer breeding birds. It is a great flier and is normally seen soaring on widely spread wings on which the primaries stand out as 'fingers'. Attention is often drawn to these birds by their high-pitched 'kee-ow' calls, of which their vernacular name is a derivative.

Habitat: Mountain or sea cliffs, quarries.

Locations: Though they breed on the cliffs of much of Wales the best spots are: Skomer and the adjacent mainland; Snowdon's slate cliffs; Isle of Man; Islay.

Jackdaw *Corvus monedula*

Resident: Jackdaws are successful birds that have benefitted greatly from the changes that man has wrought on the landscape. Gregarious at all seasons, they occupy a large range of different breeding sites from holes in trees to cathedral spires and sea cliffs. They are found in the most remote corners of the country, as well as in the centres of quite large towns. They are smallish members of the crow family and marked by a distinctive grey nape that is visible at considerable distances. Over the past hundred years or so they have spread and increased in numbers and today there may be up to 350,000 pairs in Britain.

Habitat: Grassland with adjacent woods, trees, sea cliffs, inland cliffs, cathedrals, ruins, parkland.

Locations: Common and widespread throughout Britain save for the highest and most barren parts of the Highlands. Decidedly scarce in Shetland, the Outer Hebrides (save for Stornoway Woods) and on several of the Inner Hebrides.

Rook *Corvus frugilegus*

Resident: By virtue of its gregarious nature, and particularly in forming and maintaining large colonies of nests, the rook was one of the very first landbirds to be successfully censussed in Britain. The birds return to their rookeries early in the year before the growing leaves have a chance to hide their presence and activities. They will also cling tenaciously to traditional sites, some of which have been used for a hundred or more years. In the past this conservatism has proved their undoing, for at one time farmers used to shoot up rookeries to destroy the young birds in the nest. Today, however, a more enlightened approach recognises that the birds do more good than harm and most colonies remain unmolested. Though they can be confused with the carrion crow, an experienced observer soon gets to recognise the lighter build of this species, while the bare skin at the base of the bill in the adult is diagnostic.

Habitat: Agricultural landscapes with clumps of trees or copses.

Locations: A widespread species absent only from the highest hill districts and the treeless landscapes of northernmost Scotland. Very scarce in Shetland and Outer Hebrides (Stornoway Woods); absent from Arran, parts of the Border hills, Pennines, Welsh hills and London. Largest British rookery is at Hatton Castle in Aberdeenshire where just under 7,000 nests can be found. Indeed this area of eastern Scotland has the greatest rook density in the country.

Carrion Crow *Corvus corone*

Resident: Carrion crows are resident in every part of Britain and up to three-quarters of a million pairs breed each year. They occupy a huge range of habitats from barren moorlands to city centres, and in this lies their success. Two sub-species occur in Britain and these are sufficiently distinct to merit separate vernacular names: carrion crow and hooded crow. The latter, which is the sub-species found in the north and west, has a grey rather than black body. The area of overlap and hybridization has gradually moved further north during the present century so that hooded crows are becoming progressively more scarce. Birds of this race are regular winter visitors to the east coast of England, but these are immigrants from the Continent.

Habitat: Virtually ubiquitous.

Locations: Carrion crows are found throughout England and Wales, and in Scotland north to the Great Glen and further north still in the east to Caithness. Hooded crows replace carrion crows north of the Great Glen but also extend southwards in the west as far as Kintyre and Arran. They are also the sub-species present in the Isle of Man.

Raven *Corvus corax*

Resident: Once a widespread, though apparently never common, inhabitant of most of Britain, generations of persecution have eliminated the raven from most of the lowlands. Gamekeepers have waged, and still do so, a ceaseless war against the raven, which they see as a serious predator on grouse, pheasant and partridge chicks. Even in today's more tolerant climate, keepers of grouse moors regularly destroy ravens and keep them from occupying what would otherwise be suitable territories. The birds are major scavengers in sheep districts which more or less overlap with the hilly districts of Britain. A recent slow increase has led to a greater incidence of tree nesting.

Habitat: Upland districts, moorland, sheep country, with crags and rocky outcrops, quarries mostly over 1,000 feet.

Locations: Found in Shetland; Orkney; Outer and Inner Hebrides; all over Highland Scotland; the Border hills; the Lake District and adjacent parts of the Pennines, though absent from that range further south; Isle of Man; virtually the whole of Wales; and the south-west peninsula extending eastwards along the coast of Dorset to the Isle of Wight. About 3,500 pairs breed annually.

Starling *Sturnus vulgaris*

Resident: One of the most successful of all of the world's birds. The starling has learned to live with and alongside man so well that it may now be a candidate for the 'world's most numerous bird' title. Man has introduced it to areas where it does not naturally occur with almost instant success. In Britain it has spread northwards during the present century and is now abundant to the furthest point north. It reached Iceland in 1935. An impression of its numbers may be gathered during a winter evening by watching the birds fly to roost. In huge numbers they swarm across the landscape performing complex aerial evolutions above their chosen resting place. Invariably such roosts are over-estimated in the observer's mind for most consist of less than 20,000 birds. However, larger roosts do occur, though those containing over 250,000 individuals are decidedly rare. Urban roosts, always more obvious than those in the country, usually number less than 50,000. The total breeding population is about seven million pairs.
Habitat: Virtually ubiquitous.
Locations: Abundant in every part of the country save for the highest and most desolate of Scottish hills. Largest urban roosts are in Glasgow and Bradford, with smaller roosts (under 50,000 birds) in Bristol, Birmingham, London and Newcastle.
Winter Visitor: Our resident birds are joined by huge numbers of Continental immigrants from October to March.
Locations: None specific.

House Sparrow *Passer domesticus*

Resident: Wherever man lives permanently in Britain there too he will be joined by house sparrows. Even in the remotest of mountain glens or on the most isolated of islands, this highly successful little bird will appear and survive if we are present to help. Some three to six million pairs breed with us, yet there is some evidence of a decline in numbers since the motor car replaced the horse-drawn carriage as standard transport. Certainly they must have found city centres, with their huge grain spillage, a sparrow paradise.

Habitat: Cities, towns, villages, hamlets with human occupancy; farms and agricultural land.

Locations: Absent only from the uninhabited Scottish hills and uninhabited islands. Thus present on even the isolated Fair Isle.

Tree Sparrow *Passer montanus*

Resident: About a quarter of a million pairs of tree sparrows nest in Britain, which is considerably more than one would expect, indicating that the bird is very often overlooked. While it is so similar to the male house sparrow, it does not actually require a detailed examination of every individual sparrow to find this species. It has a distinctive 'chup' call that is quite different from the 'chirrup' of the house sparrow, and always looks as if it has a white collar. The sexes are similar. As its name implies, the tree sparrow nests in holes in trees, though it also takes readily to nest boxes. It forms loose colonies up to 50 pairs strong.

Habitat: Woods, hedgerows, cliffs.

Locations: Eastern and central England remains the species' stronghold, though it has spread westwards and southwards in recent years. Today it is absent from the south-west, from Hampshire, most of western Wales, parts of the Lake District and adjacent Pennines, and most of upland Scotland and the Islands. However, it is present on the uninhabited St Kilda and North Rona; and on Fair Isle. In many areas it tends to be more of a coastal bird.

Chaffinch *Fringilla coelebs*

Resident: One of the most common and widespread of British birds with about five million pairs present, plus a huge influx of visitors from the Continent in winter. The chaffinch is really a woodland bird that finds its natural home in beech woods where the fallen mast provides plentiful winter food. It has, however, spread into a variety of other woodland habitats including conifer plantations and birch-covered moors. Over much of its range it is a common garden bird and will readily forage on or around bird tables. Its well-camouflaged nest is a masterpiece of hairs and bents covered with lichens and mosses.

Habitat: Woodland, hedgerows, parks, plantations, gardens.
Locations: In the deciduous woods of England the chaffinch is among the most common of birds. It is, however, found throughout Britain and is absent only from parts of Sutherland and Caithness, parts of the Outer Hebrides, Tiree, Col and Orkney, and from Shetland.

Brambling *Fringilla montifringilla*

Winter Visitor: The brambling probably breeds in Britain every year, though confirmation is generally lacking. This may be regarded as part of the same phenomenon that has led to the colonization of the country by other Scandinavian birds such as redwing, fieldfare and wood sandpiper in recent years. However, while these birds have moved into northern Scotland, the brambling may have bred as far south as Buckinghamshire. In general though it is a winter visitor from Scandinavia that arrives on our shores in October and departs by the end of March. It generally associates with other finches in mixed flocks, but may be found alone or with chaffinches in beech woods. When disturbed the white rump patch is often obvious, but beware confusion with the white-rumped bullfinch which seldom, however, joins in mixed flocks.
Habitat: Birch and other deciduous woods; in winter beech woods, hedgerows.
Locations: Found from southern Scotland southwards in considerable numbers, but without specific points of concentration. A good day bird-watching in January or February should locate a few bramblings.

Serin *Serinus serinus*

Summer Visitor: During the present century the serin has expanded its range northwards from the Mediterranean reaching Britain to breed for the first time in 1967. Thereafter a few pairs have bred annually, though no strong invasion or colonization has as yet taken place. Otherwise the serin remains a scarce spring and autumn visitor, attention to which is mainly drawn by its delightful tinkling song or its boldly square yellow rump. In parts of southern Europe it is one of the most common village birds and it is frequently caught and kept as a cage bird, even in areas where the birds are singing noisily outside all day long.

Habitat: Villages, orchards, large gardens, wasteland.

Locations: Most birds of passage occur in southern and especially south-western England – the Lands End peninsula is particularly favoured, at Porthgawarra for example. Breeding birds have appeared in Dorset, the New Forest, and in central Sussex, but may be looked for in any southern county.

Greenfinch *Carduelis chloris*

Resident: The greenfinch is a chunky little bird, boldly marked with green and yellow in the male, that finds a perfect home among gardens and hedgerows. Its harsh nasal call is a typical sound of spring in the suburbs, while in winter noisy flocks, often joined by other species, scour the hedgerows for food. Most British greenfinches are resident, but some make considerable migrations even abroad as far as Spain. In gardens they regularly visit bird tables and peanut dispensers and are aggressive in seeking their fair (or more than fair) share.

Habitat: Gardens, parks, orchards, hedgerows, woodland edges.

Locations: Found throughout Britian save on the highest hills in Wales, the Pennines, Galloway and the Highlands. Scarce in Orkney, Outer Hebrides (Stornoway Woods) and decidedly rare in Shetland. A total population of between one and one and a half million pairs indicates its abundance.

Goldfinch *Carduelis carduelis*

Resident: Once widely kept as cage birds, a practice still popular in the Mediterranean, goldfinches have increased considerably since this fashion died out and the species became protected by law. Yet it needs little imagination to see why this little bird was so popular. It is brightly coloured in yellow and crimson and has a delightful tinkling little song that it repeats endlessly in spring. Outside the breeding season it frequents waste ground with a plentiful supply of weeds including thistles and teasels from which it extracts the seeds with its thin pointed bill. It is usually encountered in small parties – called charms – and is often quite confiding.

Habitat: Open ground, wasteland, hedgerows, marshes, orchards, gardens.

Locations: Found over most of Britain but gradually becoming scarcer further north and virtually absent from the Scottish Highlands. Also absent from Shetland, Orkney and the Outer Hebrides. Elsewhere a comparatively easy bird to see.

Siskin *Carduelis spinus*

Resident: As recently as the middle of last century siskins were found only in the Old Caledonian forests of Scots pines. They have, however, proved as successful as any species in colonizing stands of introduced conifers, and particularly the Sitka spruce that has proved so popular with contemporary foresters. As a result they have spread, albeit thinly, to all parts of the country. They are attractive little green finches that spend almost all their time feeding in trees. They are generally gregarious and their twittering calls are a characteristic sound of areas where they are numerous. However, they may easily be confused with redpolls and may be overlooked among that more numerous species. In late winter (usually March) they have recently developed the habit of feeding in gardens on peanuts hung up for the tits and greenfinches. As a matter of preference they seem to seek out those red nylon nets that are sold in pet shops.

Habitat: Coniferous woods.

Locations: Though any area of conifers may be searched for siskins, it is the Old Caledonian pines of the Scottish Highlands that remain the species' stronghold. They are widespread throughout that region, but totally absent from the Outer Hebrides, Orkney and Shetland. They are widespread in the Border country, but elsewhere rather scarce. The Brecks and north-west Wales are the only concentration points.

Winter Visitor: Immigrants arrive on the east coast in September and October and quickly spread through the country.

Locations: None specific.

Linnet *Carduelis cannabina*

Resident: Twittering flocks of linnets are as familiar to the countryman as virtually any other bird. They inhabit every type of open landscape and feed, predominantly on the ground, on the fallen seeds of a wide variety of weeds. During the breeding season they will take to bushes or heaths, hedgerows, woodland edges and gardens, but even at this season they remain gregarious, breeding in small colonies and foraging in small flocks. At other times of the year flocks may become very large and on suitable coastal marshes a thousand or more may be found together. The red on the breast of the male identifies it at all seasons and there is a flash of white on the tail and wings in flight. Care must be taken in separating twite and linnet in winter.

Habitat: Open heaths, hedgerows, shore marshes, parks, conifer plantations, scrub and wasteland.

Locations: Over a million pairs breed in Britain where it is present throughout the country save for the Highlands, Shetlands and most of the Outer Hebrides. In these areas it is largely replaced by the twite.

Twite *Carduelis flavirostris*

Resident: This rather nondescript little finch inhabits open moorland from the high hills in the south of its range down to shorelands in the north. Though it more or less replaces the linnet in this habitat, the separation is not complete and the two may be found very close together in some parts of the country. It is best identified by its lack of red on the head and breast in all plumages, and by its pale bill. Its usual call note is very similar to that of the linnet, making separation in winter flocks a particular problem. The vinous rump stressed in so many identification guides is useless in the field.

Habitat: Open moorland of grass and heather, often with stone walls.

Locations: Coastal northern Scotland – Shetland, Orkney and Outer Hebrides, Caithness, Sutherland and Wester Ross are the strongholds. There are smaller populations inland among the Highlands and in the central Pennines. Winter flocks on the east coast, particularly in East Anglia at Gibraltar Point, Cley, and Walberswick, are native birds.

Redpoll *Carduelis flammea*

Resident: There can be no doubt that the redpoll is far more numerous today than at any time during the past hundred years. Its preferred habitat of birch, willow and alder scrub has increased considerably with the planting of these species in many areas and redpolls have increased and spread as a result. Though they seem nondescript little brown birds as they cling tit-like to a catkin while feeding, in flight their characteristic nasal calls are both far-carrying and diagnostic. Given decent views the small black bib and crimson patch on the crown are sufficient to separate it from any other species save the arctic redpoll, which is a very rare visitor, mainly to Fair Isle. Like other members of the genus, redpolls are gregarious little birds that even nest in loose colonies. They are essentially arboreal, however, and do not join the mixed finch flocks on coastal marshes.

Habitat: Birch, willow and alder scrub and woodland; also conifers.
Locations: Common over northern and eastern England and over most of Scotland, but absent from the Outer Hebrides (save Stornoway Woods), Orkney, Shetland and parts of Caithness. It is missing from the Fens and is decidedly local in central and south England and the south-west. However, an expanding population means that the species can be looked for anywhere.

Crossbill *Loxia curvirostra*

Resident: The crossbill is the most specifically adapted of all British birds. Its overlapping mandibles are used to prise open the blades of pine cones and extract the seeds with its tongue. Such an adaptation has the obvious advantage of enabling the species to exploit a food source that is unavailable to other birds. But it also contains the element of a possible disaster should the conifer crop fail. Different populations of crossbills have different-sized cones to deal with, depending on the dominant species of tree. Those in Scotland, living on Scots pine, have heavier bills than many Continental birds, and have been recognised as a separate sub-species *L.c. scotica* (sometimes even as a distinct species) as a result. Dependence on a single food source means that crop failure sends whole populations of crossbills migrating in their search for suitable forests. In such years large numbers of birds may arrive in Britain and even settle down to breed in subsequent years. Since 1910 there have been populations in the Brecks and New Forest, and with larger areas of planted conifers available many small crossbill populations now exist in England.

Habitat: Coniferous forests.

Locations: The native Scottish crossbill is confined to the Old Caledonian forests of the Highlands such as Rothiemurchus and Abernethy, and to adjacent more recent plantations. The Brecks and New Forest have established populations of the typical crossbill and, following irruptions in the early 1960s, these birds now breed in many parts of southern and eastern England.

Bullfinch *Pyrrhula pyrrhula*

Resident: Although such an attractive member of the British avifauna, the male having a resplendent bright pink breast, the bullfinch is far from popular in many parts of the country. The reasons for this are not hard to find. Dependent for its winter survival on the seeds of ash trees, the failure of this food source in early spring sends the birds scurrying off to the nearest orchard where growing fruit buds form an excellent alternative. This means that the crop of fruits such as apples, cherries, plums and pears can be drastically reduced even before they start to grow. As a result the bullfinch is not protected by law and is trapped and killed in many areas. Fortunately this has little appreciable effect on its population which is estimated at approaching half a million pairs. Unlike so many other finches, these birds are seldom found other than in pairs or family parties. Their square white rump is easily seen as they flit away along some hedgerow.

Habitat: Woodland edge, scrub, hedgerows, gardens, orchards, young plantations.

Locations: Present over most of Britain save for parts of the Fens, the Welsh hills, parts of the Pennines and Border hills, and large treeless areas of the Highlands and Islands. Absent from Shetland, Orkney, Outer Hebrides and Isle of Man.

Hawfinch *Coccothraustes coccothraustes*

Resident: Confined to south-east England until the middle of last century, the hawfinch has expanded its range both northwards and westwards over the last hundred years. Despite what can only be an increase in numbers, the species remains one of the most elusive of all our resident birds. Estimates of 5,000 – 10,000 breeding pairs do little to indicate the true difficulties involved in seeing this bird, though in parts of Continental Europe it is both numerous and approachable. The distinctive flight silhouette, with large head and chunky body, coupled with the strong 'tik' flight note are worth remembering, for a single glance may be all that one gets, even in an area that is noted for their presence. Like so many other finches they are at least semi-colonial, and the presence of an individual at any season makes an area always worthy of a subsequent look by virtue of its tendency to remain strictly resident. The huge, thick bill is diagnostic at all seasons.

Habitat: Deciduous woods with beech, sycamore, wild cherry, hornbeam, etc; also cherry orchards.

Locations: Virtually absent from Scotland, Wales and south-western England. Best looked for in the 'Home Counties'. Virginia Water is a known haunt as is Kew Gardens in London.

Lapland Bunting *Calcarius lapponicus*

Resident: As recently as 1977 the Lapland bunting could be classed only as a scarce passage migrant and winter visitor. Then no less than 14 separate pairs were found at 6 distinct sites in Scotland, and some of these nested successfully. No doubt the extreme lateness of the season was at least partly responsible, but the gradual climatic change that has brought so many other Scandinavian species to our shores may also be involved, in which case a more permanent colonization may result.

Habitat: Barren mountain tops and screes; at other seasons mainly shorelines and coastal marshes.

Locations: Highland Scotland.

Passage Migrant: The most usual occurrences of Lapland buntings are as autumn migrants from September to early November in Shetland and the east and south coasts. Only small numbers are involved and a flock of 10 or more is quite noteworthy.

Locations: Regular spots are difficult to list, but the Cley, Blakeney and Morston area of north Norfolk is one. Winter visitors are decidedly scarce.

Snow Bunting *Plectrophenax nivalis*

Resident: Small numbers of snow buntings regularly nest on the highest of Scottish mountains, with the centre of distribution clearly in the Cairngorm—Grampian massif. In 1977 a particularly late spring induced many more than usual to stay and a possible 15 pairs that year represent roughly double the usual number.

Habitat: Open barren mountain tops; in winter along beaches and coastal marshes.

Locations: Cairngorms—Grampians; several of the highest mountains north-west of the Caledonian Canal.

Winter Visitor: Flocks of snow buntings build up along the north, west and east coasts of Britain during October and stay to winter there and inland on Scottish mountains.

Locations: They are decidedly scarce in the south and west, and largest flocks are often present in North Norfolk at Cley and Blakeney. Usually seen in groups of 10 to 20, but up to 500 at favoured spots.

Yellowhammer *Emberiza citrinella*

Resident: A widespread and numerous member of our avifauna being particularly abundant along hedgerows and on heaths bordering agricultural land. Its bright yellow colouring and characteristic song, often rendered as 'little-bit-of-bread-and-no-cheese' are known even to the mass of the population, and it is regarded with great affection by all country folk. A recently noted decline has been attributed to the ripping out of hedgerows and the use of agricultural chemicals, but there is no evidence that this is either serious or lasting.

Habitat: Hedgerows, heaths, commons, woodland edge, scrub, young conifer plantations.

Locations: Widespread, but absent from London, parts of the Pennines, the highest parts of the Border country, and much of the Scottish Highlands, the Outer Hebrides (save for Stornoway Woods), most of Orkney and all of Shetland. Winter visitors from the Continent may occupy the east coast, even bringing birds to Shetland where they do not nest.

Cirl Bunting *Emberiza cirlus*

Resident: No more than 700 pairs of this very attractive bunting nest in Britain each year, and the species remains one of the most elusive of residents for which the bird-watcher must search. It is not a widespread species, breeding only in western and Mediterranean Europe eastwards into Turkey. It finds in England, however, its most northern limit and penetrates no further than the south Midlands. It is a bird of sheltered valleys of agricultural land where there are hedgerows with trees such as elms. The foot of southern sloping hills, especially around the outskirts of villages, are particularly favoured. Its rattling song is a sure means of location in suitable areas.

Habitat: Hedgerows and copses at the foot of south facing hills as well as similarly situated gullies.

Locations: The foot of the South Downs westwards from Beachy Head; the south Devon coast from Exe to Prawle Point; and other spots south of a line from Bristol to London.

Ortolan Bunting *Emberiza hortulana*

Passage Migrant: A small number of these attractive buntings reach our shores every autumn and even smaller numbers in spring. They are generally found on arable fields, where they are easily overlooked, and seldom far from the coast. Spring records away from Fair Isle are exceptional. Most autumn records are in September with a scattering in August, October and November. Even at this season Fair Isle remains dominant, together with that other outstanding haunt of birds and their watchers, the north coast of Norfolk. This concentration at what are arguably the two most heavily watched areas in Britain indicates not that ortolans concentrate at places frequented by bird-watchers or the reverse, but rather that they are overlooked elsewhere. Occasionally more than one occurs and even small flocks are not unknown.

Habitat: Cultivated land with trees, hedges, walls, etc; often on plough.

Locations: Probably overlooked at many coastal sites especially on the east coast; regular at Fair Isle, North Norfolk and becoming so on Isles of Scilly.

Reed Bunting *Emberiza schoeniclus*

Resident: For reasons that remain purely speculative reed buntings, which are primarily birds of marsh or at least wetland habitats, have moved into drier zones to occupy areas that would generally be regarded as more suitable to yellowhammers. Along with this move they have also spread and colonized regions where they were previously unknown. There can be little doubt that in terms of actual numbers the species has increased considerably over the last few years and that the move into dry regions is at least in part a move into a marginal habitat as far as reed buntings are concerned. Whatever the causes, this attractive bird can now be found even in gardens and along hedgerows.
Habitat: Marshes, riverside vegetation, floods, also scrub, hedgerows and large gardens.
Locations: Approaching half a million pairs of reed buntings breed in Britain making the species one of the more common of our birds. It is widespread from Shetland (colonized 1949) to Land's End and is absent only from the hilly districts. Largest numbers are to be found in central and eastern England, but there is hardly a decent-sized reed bed in the country that does not have a healthy population.

Corn Bunting *Miliaria calandra*

Resident: For generations ornithologists have puzzled over the truly strange distribution of the corn bunting. In some areas it is abundant, though never to the level that it can be found, for instance, in many parts of the Mediterranean. In other areas it is simply absent. If habitat seems the most likely key, then it is a complex one, and fits a highly complex lock. Arable land with hedgerows seems essential, but it also needs isolated bushes, or fences, or telegraph wires from which to sing its jingling little song. Such conditions are found over large areas of central Norfolk and Suffolk, but corn buntings are totally absent. They are also absent from hilly districts and from the wetter areas of the west, except for the coast of north Cornwall and the dune country of the Outer Hebrides where they are common. The corn bunting remains an enigma.
Habitat: Arable land with plentiful song posts.

Locations: The central and eastern parts of the country have the best populations of corn buntings and the hilly districts the poorest. They are also absent from the west save for Cornwall and the Outer Hebrides. There are many other unexplained patches in this bird's British distribution.

RARITIES

Every species on the British and Irish List has been covered in the main text, with the exception of those that have occurred so infrequently that no pattern emerges that could prove useful to the bird-seeker, or those which have occurred only in Ireland. These 'rare' birds are listed below together with the total number of records, and direction of origin, as at 1st January 1979.

Pied-billed Grebe *Podilymbus podiceps*: First recorded 1963; a handful of records probably of 3 birds; North America.

Black-browed Albatross *Diomedea melanophris*: 22 records including a regular bird at gannetries on the Bass Rock and Shetland between 1967 and 1979; southern oceans.

Capped Petrel *Pterodroma hasitata*: 1 record 1850; West Indies.

Bulwer's Petrel *Bulweria bulwerii*: 2 records 1837 and 1908; Atlantic islands.

Little Shearwater *Puffinus assimilis*: a handful of dead or dying birds but regular off south-western Ireland; Atlantic islands.

Wilson's Petrel *Oceanites oceanicus*: a handful of records (3 in Cornwall); Antarctic.

Frigate Petrel (White-faced Petrel) *Pelagodroma marina*: 1 record 1897.

Madeiran Petrel *Oceanodroma castro*: 2 records 1911 and 1931.

Magnificent Frigatebird *Fregata magnificens*: 1 record plus 1 or 2 others of frigatebirds not specifically identified; tropical Atlantic.

American Bittern *Botaurus lentiginosus*: 55 records; North America.

Green Heron *Butorides striatus*: 1 record 1889; cosmopolitan.

Squacco Heron *Ardeola ralloides*: less than 1 record a year; southern Europe.

Cattle Egret *Bulbulcus ibis*: less than 1 record a year, but many others treated as escapes; resident southern Europe.

Great White Egret *Egretta alba*: 17 records; south-eastern Europe.

Black Stork *Ciconia nigra*: 42 records but may have been escapes; southern Europe.

White Stork *Ciconia ciconia*: 245 records many of which have probably been escapes; southern and eastern Europe.

Glossy Ibis *Plegadis falcinellus*: vagrant and possible escape, formerly more regular; south-eastern Europe.

Red-breasted Goose *Branta ruficollis*: 25 records mostly Slimbridge; south-eastern Europe.

Ruddy Shelduck *Tadorna ferruginea*: old wild records, recent ones mostly escapes; south-eastern Europe.

American Wigeon *Anas americana*: 104 records; North America.

Falcated Duck *Anas falcata*: 1 record recently accepted on British List; Asia.

Black Duck *Anas rubripes*: 8 records, all since species has been kept in captivity; North America.

Blue-winged Teal *Anas discors*: 71 records, many genuine; North America.

Ring-necked Duck *Aythya collaris*: irregular in winter; North America.

Harlequin Duck *Histrionicus histrionicus*: a handful of records; Iceland, North America.

Bufflehead *Bucephala albeola*: very rare; North America.

Hooded Merganser *Mergus cucullatus*: a handful of records; North America.

Black Kite *Milvus migrans*: 30 records; southern Europe.

Egyptian Vulture *Neophron percnopterus*: 2 old records; southern Europe.

Griffon Vulture *Gyps fulvus*: 2 old records; southern Europe.

Pallid Harrier *Circus macrourus*: 3 records; eastern Europe.

Spotted Eagle *Aquila clanga*: 12 old records; south-eastern Europe.

Lesser Kestrel *Falco naumanni*: highly irregular; southern Europe.

American Kestrel *Falco sparverius*: 2 records; North America

Eleonora's Falcon *Falco eleonorae*: 1 record 1977; Mediterranean.

Sora Rail *Porzana carolina*: a handful of records; North America.

Little Crake *Porzana parva*: about 1 record a year; eastern Europe.

Baillon's Crake *Porzana pusilla*: declining number of records; southern Europe.

Allen's Gallinule *Porphyrula alleni*: 1 record 1902; North Africa.

American Purple Gallinule *Porphyrula martinica*: 1 record 1958; North America.

Common Crane *Grus grus*: a few each year, influx in 1963; northern Europe.

Sandhill Crane *Grus canadensis*: 1 record 1905; North America.

Little Bustard *Tetrax tetrax*: less than 1 record a year; southern Europe.

Houbara Bustard *Chlamydotis undulata*: 5 records; North Africa and Middle East.

Great Bustard *Otis tarda*: 3 or 4 records each decade, attempted reintroduction on Salisbury Plain; southern and eastern Europe.

Black-winged Stilt *Himantopus himantopus*: averages more than one a year with occasional influxes; southern Europe.

Cream-coloured Courser *Cursorius cursor*: less than 1 record a year; North Africa.

Collared Pratincole *Glareola pratincola*: a handful of records each year, mostly spring; southern Europe.

Black-winged Pratincole *Glareola nordmanni*: a couple of records each year, mostly autumn; eastern Europe.

Semi-palmated Plover *Charadrius semipalmatus*: 1 record 1978; North America.

Killdeer *Charadrius vociferus*: less than one record a year; North America.

Caspian Plover *Charadrius asiaticus*: 1 record 1890; Asia.

Lesser Golden Plover *Pluvialis dominica*: increasingly recorded, now annual; North America.

Sociable Plover *Vanellus gregarius*: about 1 record a year; Siberia.

Semi-palmated Sandpiper *Calidris pusilla*: 6 records acceptable, but many others claimed; great identification difficulties; North America.

Western Sandpiper *Calidris mauri*: highly irregular; North America.

Least Sandpiper *Calidris minutilla*: about 1 record a year; North America.

White-rumped Sandpiper *Calidris fuscicollis*: a handful each autumn; North America.

Baird's Sandpiper *Calidris bairdii*: a couple of records each autumn; North America.

Sharp-tailed Sandpiper *Calidris acuminata*: irregular but increasing; Siberia.

Broad-billed Sandpiper *Limicola falcinellus*: very irregular; northern Europe.

Stilt Sandpiper *Micropalama himantopus*: a handful of records; North America.

Buff-breasted Sandpiper *Tryngites subruficollis*: increasingly regular in autumn; North America.

Great Snipe *Gallinago media*: declining vagrant at all seasons with only 1 or 2 a year; northern Europe.

Short-billed Dowitcher *Limnodromus griseus*: very rare, but most dowitchers are not specifically identified; North America.

Long-billed Dowitcher *Limnodromus scolopaceus*: slightly more numerous of the 2 dowitchers; North America.

Eskimo Curlew *Numenius borealis*: old records only, virtually extinct; North America.

Upland Sandpiper *Bartramia longicauda*: 1 or 2 most years; North America.

Marsh Sandpiper *Tringa stagnatilis*: very irregular; eastern Europe.

Greater Yellowlegs *Tringa melanoleuca*: 23 records; North America.

Lesser Yellowlegs *Tringa flavipes*: between 1 and 8 each year; North America.

Solitary Sandpiper *Tringa solitaria*: very irregular; North America.

Terek Sandpiper *Xenus cinereus*: 17 records; northern Europe and Siberia.

Spotted Sandpiper *Actitis macularia*: irregular but increasingly recorded; North America.

Wilson's Phalarope *Phalaropus tricolor*: increasingly recorded with a handful most years; North America.

Laughing Gull *Larus atricilla*: 19 records, but perhaps increasingly identified; North America.

Franklin's Gull *Larus pipixcan*: 5 records; North America.

Bonaparte's Gull *Larus philadelphia*: very irregular; North America.

Slender-billed Gull *Larus genei*: a handful of records; Mediterranean.

Ring-billed Gull *Larus delawarensis*: 22 records, but increasingly identified at Blackpill, Swansea Bay; North America.

Ross's Gull *Rhodostethia rosea*: 22 records, but increasingly sought after and identified; Arctic.

Royal Tern *Sterna maxima*: highly irregular; tropical Atlantic.

Bridled Tern *Sterna anaethetus*: 5 records all found dead; tropical Atlantic.

Sooty Tern *Sterna fuscata*: very irregular, usually found dead; tropical Atlantic.

Brunnich's Guillemot *Uria lomvia*: 10 records all but 1 found dead; Arctic.

Pallas's Sandgrouse *Syrrhaptes paradoxus*: formerly irruptive, now very irregular; southern Siberia.

Rufous Turtle Dove *Streptopelia orientalis*: 8 records; Asia.

Great Spotted Cuckoo *Clamator glandarius*: 21 records; southern Europe.

Black-billed Cuckoo *Coccyzus erythropthalmus*: highly irregular; North America.

Yellow-billed Cuckoo *Coccyzus americanus*: 35 records; North America.

Scops Owl *Otus scops*: highly irregular, though formerly more numerous; southern Europe.

Eagle Owl *Bubo bubo*: last seen 1883; southern and eastern Europe.

Hawk Owl *Surnia ulula*: highly irregular; Scandinavia and North America.

Tengmalm's Owl *Aegolius funereus*: once more frequent but now highly irregular; Scandinavia.

Red-necked Nightjar *Caprimulgus ruficollis*: 1 record 1856; southern Europe.

Egyptian Nightjar *Caprimulgus aegyptius*: 1 record 1883; North Africa.

Common Nighthawk *Chordeiles minor*: 8 records; North America.

Needle-tailed Swift *Hirundapus caudacutus*: 2 records last century; Asia.

Alpine Swift *Apus melba*: a handful each year; southern Europe.

Little Swift *Apus affinis*: 1 record; North Africa and Asia.

Blue-cheeked Bee-eater *Merops superciliosus*: 2 records; North Africa.

Bee-eater *Merops apiaster*: a handful each spring, rarer in autumn, has bred; southern Europe.

Roller *Coracias garrulus*: a few most years; southern Europe.

Yellow-bellied Sapsucker *Sphyrapicus varius*: 1 record 1975; North America.

Calandra Lark *Melanocorypha calandra*: 2 records 1961 and 1978; southern Europe.

Bimaculated Lark *Melanocorypha bimaculata*: exceptionally rare; Middle East.

White-winged Lark *Melanocorypha leucoptera*: 4 records pre-1955; southern Siberia.

Short-toed Lark *Calandrella brachydactyla*: from 1 to 12 each year; southern Europe.

Crested Lark *Galerida cristata*: may yet be proved to breed, otherwise highly irregular; Continental Europe.

Red-rumped Swallow *Hirundo daurica*: gradually becoming an annual spring and irregular autumn vagrant; southern Europe.

Tawny Pipit *Anthus campestris*: regular autumn migrant in varying numbers up to 25 a year; Continental Europe.

Olive-backed Pipit *Anthus hodgsoni*: handful of records of highly irregular vagrant; Asia.

Pechora Pipit *Anthus gustavi*: highly irregular at Fair Isle; Siberia.

Red-throated Pipit *Anthus cervinus*: 1 or 2 most years; Scandinavia.

Citrine Wagtail *Motacilla citreola*: 1 or 2 each autumn; Asia.

Brown Thrasher *Toxostoma rufum*: 1 record 1966–1967; North America.

Alpine Accentor *Prunella collaris*: very scarce, formerly more regular; Continental Europe.

Rufous Bush Chat *Cercotrichas galactotes*: highly irregular; southern Europe.

Thrush Nightingale *Luscinia luscinia*: irregular, but perhaps increasing; eastern Europe.

Siberian Rubythroat *Luscinia calliope*: 1 Fair Isle 1975, 1 Lincolnshire 1977; Siberia.

Red-flanked Bluetail *Tasiger cyanurus*: 8 records; Finland eastwards.

Isabelline Wheatear *Oenanthe isabellina*: a handful of records; south-eastern Europe.

Pied Wheatear *Oenanthe pleschanka*: 6 records; south-eastern Europe.

Black-eared Wheatear *Oenanthe hispanica*: highly irregular; southern Europe.

Desert Wheatear *Oenanthe deserti*: 21 records; North Africa.

Black Wheatear *Oenanthe leucura*: a handful of records; southern Europe.

Rock Thrush *Monticola saxatilis*: highly irregular; southern Europe.

White's Thrush *Zoothera dauma*: highly irregular, though formerly more frequent; Siberia.

Siberian Thrush *Zoothera sibiricus*: 1 record 1954; Siberia.

Hermit Thrush *Catharus guttatus*: 1 record 1975; North America.

Grey-cheeked Thrush *Catharus minimus*: a handful of recent records only; North America.

Veery *Catharus fuscescens*: 1 record 1970; North America.

Eye-browed Thrush *Turdus obscurus*: 4 records, 3 in 1964; North America.

Dusky Thrush *Turdus naumanni*: a handful of records; Siberia.

Black-throated Thrush *Turdus ruficollis*: 9 records; Siberia.

American Robin *Turdus migratorius*: very irregular; North America.

Pallas's Grasshopper Warbler *Locustella certhiola*: 5 records; Siberia.

Lanceolated Warbler *Locustella lanceolata*: 26 records mostly at Fair Isle; Siberia.

River Warbler *Locustella fluviatilis*: a handful of records; eastern Europe.

Moustached Warbler *Acrocephalus melanopogon*: a handful of records including one of breeding in Cambridgeshire in 1946; southern and eastern Europe.

Aquatic Warbler *Acrocephalus paludicola*: regularly up to 40 each autumn

(August – September) and increasing – Slapton Ley and Dorset coast do best; eastern and south-eastern Europe.

Paddyfield Warbler *Acrocephalus agricola*: a handful of records; Siberia.

Blyth's Reed Warbler *Acrocephalus dumetorum*: highly irregular; Finland eastwards.

Great Reed Warbler *Acrocephalus arundinaceus*: up to a half a dozen most years in May and June; southern Europe.

Thick-billed Warbler *Acrocephalus aedon*: a few records at Fair Isle; Siberia.

Olivaceous Warbler *Hippolais pallida*: highly irregular in autumn; southern Europe.

Booted Warbler *Hippolais caligata*: 10 records; southern Siberia and Middle East.

Spectacled Warbler *Sylvia conspicillata*: a few records; Mediterranean.

Subalpine Warbler *Sylvia cantillans*: 1 to 4 most springs, irregular in autumn; Mediterranean.

Sardinian Warbler *Sylvia melanocephala*: 5 records mostly recent; Mediterranean.

Rüppell's Warbler *Sylvia rueppelli*: 1 record Shetland 1977; eastern Mediterranean.

Desert Warbler *Sylvia nana*: a handful of records since 1971; North Africa.

Orphean Warbler *Sylvia hortensis*: a handful of records; Mediterranean.

Greenish Warbler *Phylloscopus trochiloides*: regular in small numbers each autumn and occasionally winters; Finland and eastern Europe.

Arctic Warbler *Phylloscopus borealis*: 2 to 8 each autumn; Lapland eastwards.

Pallas's Warbler *Phylloscopus proregulus*: Up to 29 each autumn, usually a handful, at the end of October; Siberia.

Yellow-browed Warbler *Phylloscopus inornatus*: a handful each autumn usually in late September to mid-October; northern Siberia.

Radde's Warbler *Phylloscopus schwarzi*: 25 records; Siberia.

Dusky Warbler *Phylloscopus fuscatus*: 25 records in late October to mid-November; Siberia.

Bonelli's Warbler *Phylloscopus bonelli*: irregular in spring, up to 6 in autumn; southern Europe.

Red-breasted Flycatcher *Ficedula parva*: regular every autumn in small numbers; eastern Europe.

Collared Flycatcher *Ficedula albicollis*: highly irregular; eastern Europe.

Wallcreeper *Tichodroma muraria*: 9 records; alpine Europe.

Short-toed Treecreeper *Certhia brachydactyla*: 7 records, undetermined status due to difficulties of identification; Continental Europe.

Penduline Tit *Remiz pendulinus*: 2 records 1966 and 1977.

Isabelline Shrike *Lanius isabellinus*: 13 records; Asia.

Lesser Grey Shrike *Lanius minor*: regular in small numbers each spring (May – June) and less so in autumn (September – October); southern and south-eastern Europe.

Woodchat Shrike *Lanius senator*: from 1 to 12 each year, more in spring (May –
June) than autumn; southern Europe.

Nutcracker *Nucifraga caryocatactes*: highly irregular with occasional irruptions when several hundred may be present; Siberia.

Rose-coloured Starling *Sturnus roseus*: a handful most years, usually June to
September; eastern Europe.

Spanish Sparrow *Passer hispaniolensis*: a couple of records; Mediterranean.

Red-eyed Vireo *Vireo olivaceus*: 10 records mainly in first half of October in Isles
of Scilly; North America.

Citril Finch *Serinus citrinella*: 1 record 1904; alpine Europe.

Arctic Redpoll *Carduelis hornemanni*: irregular visitor with occasional influxes
of minor irruptive nature; Scandinavia and northern Siberia.

Two-barred Crossbill *Loxia leucoptera*: irregular visitor with 'influxes' of up to
7 birds in a year; Scandinavia and northern Siberia.

Parrot Crossbill *Loxia pytyopsittacus*: irregular visitor with crossbill invasions;
Scandinavia and northern Siberia.

Trumpeter Finch *Rhodopechys githaginea*: 2 records both 1971; North Africa
and more recently Spain.

Scarlet Rosefinch *Carpodacus erythrinus*: increasing numbers every year
mostly in August and September with vast majority on Fair Isle; eastern
Europe eastwards.

Pine Grosbeak *Pinicola enucleator*: very irregular; Scandinavia and northern
Siberia.

Evening Grosbeak *Hesperiphona vespertina*: first recorded 1969; North
America.

Black and White Warbler *Mniotilta varia*: 4 records; North America.

Tennessee Warbler *Vermivora peregrina*: 2 records both 1975 at Fair Isle;
North America.

Parula Warbler *Parula americana*: 3 records; North America.

Yellow Warbler *Dendroica petechia*: 1 record 1964; North America.

Cape May Warbler *Dendroica tigrina*: 1 record Paisley 1977; North America.

Yellow-rumped Warbler *Dendroica coronata*: 4 records; North America. Also
called myrtle warbler.

Blackpoll Warbler *Dendroica striata*: 3 records; North America.

American Redstart *Setophaga ruticilla*: 1 record 1967; North America.

Ovenbird *Seirus aurocapillus*: 1 record 1973; North America.

Northern Waterthrush *Seirus noveboracensis*: 2 records both Isles of Scilly 1958
and 1968; North America.

Yellowthroat *Geothylpis trichas*: 1 record 1954; North America.

Hooded Warbler *Wilsonia citrina*: 1 record 1970; North America.

Summer Tanager *Piranga rubra*: 1 record 1957; North America.

Scarlet Tanager *Piranga olivacea*: 2 records both Isles of Scilly; North America.

Rufous-sided Towhee *Pipilo erythropthalmus*: 2 records 1966 and 1976; North
America.

Song Sparrow *Zonotrichia melodia*: 4 records in April-May; North America.
White-crowned Sparrow *Zonotrichia leucophrys*: 2 records 1977; North America.
White-throated Sparrow *Zonotrichia albicollis*: 11 records; North America.
Slate-coloured Junco *Junco hyemalis*: a handful of records; North America.
Pine Bunting *Emberiza leucocephalos*: a handful of records; Siberia.
Rock Bunting *Emberiza cia*: a handful of records; Mediterranean.
Cretzschmar's Bunting *Emberiza caesia*: 1 record 1967; eastern Mediterranean.
Rustic Bunting *Emberiza rustica*: a handful in spring at Fair Isle (May and early June) and again in autumn (September and October) when there are also a few at Isles of Scilly; Scandinavia and northern Siberia.
Little Bunting *Emberiza pusilla*: 1 to 10 each year mostly Fair Isle in autumn (September to October); Scandinavia and northern Siberia.
Yellow-breasted Bunting *Emberiza aureola*: increasingly recorded though only a handful each year mainly September at Fair Isle; Finland eastwards.
Pallas's Reed Bunting *Emberiza pallasi* 1 record Fair Isle 1976; Siberia.
Black-headed Bunting *Emberiza melanocephala*: 1 or 2 most years in May or June mostly Fair Isle; south-eastern Europe.
Rose-breasted Grosbeak *Pheucticus ludovicianus*: 2 records 1966 and 1967; North America.
Bobolink *Dolichonyx oryzivorus*: a handful of records; North America.
Northern Oriole *Icterus galbula*: very irregular mostly south-west; North America.

GAZETTEER

All locations mentioned in the text are listed alphabetically below. Those printed in italics have merited an entry in my book *Where to Watch Birds*, also published in hardback by André Deutsch, to the index of which readers are referred. All other locations are specified, usually to the nearest large town, though some are included with other spots in *Where to Watch Birds* (WWB), in which case a 'WWB' is followed by the main place name.

Chilterns, Aylesbury, Buckinghamshire
Chittening Worth, WWB Guscar Rocks
Christchurch Harbour
Cley, see Hot Spots
Clo Mor
Cobbinshaw Reservoir
Cobham, west of Epsom, Surrey
Colne Estuary, south of Colchester, Essex
Coquet Island, off Alnwick, Northumberland
Cotswold Water Park, Cirencester, Gloucestershire
Covehithe Broad
Crag Lough, WWB Grindon Lough
Cromarty Firth
Crouch Estuary, WWB Foulness
Culbin
Dartmoor
Datchet Reservoir, east of Windsor, London
Dawlish Warren
Dee Estuary
Dengie Flats
Derwent Floods
Dornoch Firth
Druidibeg, Loch
Duddingston Loch
Duddon Estuary
Duncansby Head, John o' Groats, Caithness
Dungeness, see Hot Spots
Dunnet Head
Dunwich, WWB Minsmere
Durlston Head
Eccup Reservoir
Eden Estuary
Eigg, Isle of, south of Skye
Elie Ness
Ellesmere
Elveden, Suffolk
Exe Estuary
Eyebrook Reservoir
Fairburn Ings
Fair Isle, see Hot Spots

Farlington Marsh
Farne Islands
Farrar, Glen, Highland
Fawley, 14 miles south of Southampton, Hampshire
Fetlar
Fidra
Flamborough Head
Flanders Moss
Flannan Isles
Flatholm
Fleet, Loch
Forth, Firth of, WWB Seafield, Leith, Lothian
Forvie, Sands of
Foula, Shetland
Foulness
Foulney Island
Fowlmere, Bury St. Edmunds, Suffolk
Fowlsheugh
Frampton-on-Severn
Garten, Loch
Gibraltar Point, see Hot Spots
Gigha, WWB West Loch Tarbert
Gins, The
Gladhouse Reservoir
Glen More
Grafham Water
Grampians, border between Highland and Tayside
Grassholm
Great Ormes Head
Greenlee Lough, WWB Grindon Lough
Grindon Lough
Gruinart, Loch, WWB Islay
Gullane Bay, Firth of Forth
Guscar Rocks
Hamford Water, WWB Walton-on-the-Naze
Handa
Hanningfield Reservoir
Harewood
Harray, Loch
Hartlepool, Durham
Havergate Island

Hayle Estuary
Hermaness, WWB Unst
Hickling Broad
Hilbre
Holkham, see Hot Spots
Holme, see Hot Spots
Hornsea Mere
Horse Island
Hoy
Hule Moss
Humber Estuary, WWB Humber
  Wildfowl Refuge
Hurworth Burn
Inchmickery
Indaal, Loch, WWB Islay
Islay
Ken, Loch
Keyhaven
Kilconquhar Loch
King George V Reservoir, Enfield,
  London
Kingsbridge Estuary
Kintyre, WWB West Loch Tarbert
Kinveachy, Invernesshire
Kirkconnel, Dumfriesshire
Kylesku
Langstone Harbour
Lark, River, WWB Breckland
Leigh, Southend, Essex
Leighton Moss
Leith, WWB Seafield
Leven, Loch
Lindisfarne
Lintrathen, Loch of
Livermere, WWB Brecks
Lizard, The, south of Falmouth,
  Cornwall
Lochinch
Lundy Island
Lyme Regis, Dorset
Man, Calf of
Mar, west of Braemar, Grampian
Marazion Marsh
Maree, Loch, Gairloch, Highland
Marlborough Downs
Martin Mere
Marwick Head

Maulden Woods, near Biggleswade,
  Bedfordshire
May, Isle of, see Hot Spots
Medway Estuary
Mentieth, Loch of
Mentmore, Buckinghamshire
Mersey Estuary
Micklemere, Bury St. Edmunds,
  Suffolk
Millom, WWB Duddon Estuary
Minsmere
Mole, River, Leatherhead, Surrey
Monadliath, Kingussie, Highland
Monarch Isles, WWB Berneray
Montrose Basin
Moray Firth, Highland
Morecambe Bay
Moricambe Bay
Morlich, Loch, WWB
  Rothiemurchus
Narford Lake, Thetford, Norfolk
Needles, Isle of Wight
Needs Oar Point
Nene Washes, March,
  Huntingdonshire
Newmarket Heath, Cambridgeshire
New Forest
Newtown Marsh
North Foreland, Margate, Kent
North Kent Marshes, WWB Cliffe
North Rona, WWB Berneray
Noss (Shetland)
Orfordness, WWB Havergate
Oronsay, west of Jura
Ouse Washes, see Hot Spots
Oxwich Bay
Pagham Harbour
Papa Westray, WWB Westray
Pennan Head
Pevensey Bay, north of Eastbourne,
  Sussex
Pitsford Reservoir
Poole Harbour
Porthgawarra, Penzance, Cornwall
Portland Bill, see Hot Spots
Puffin Island
Queen Mary Reservoir

Queen Mother Reservoir, Sunbury, London
Radipole
Rannoch, Highland
Ravenglass
Rescobie, Loch, east of Forfar, Tayside
Rhum, Isle of
Rockcliffe
Rostherne Mere
Rothiemurchus
Rough Firth
Rutland Water, 20 miles east of Leicester
Rye Harbour
St Abb's Head
St Agnes
St Bee's Head
St Ives Island, see Hot Spots
St Kilda
Sandwich Bay
Scilly, Isles of, see Hot Spots
Scolt Head Island
Seahouses
Selsey Bill
Sheppey, Isle of, see Hot Spots
Shiant Islands
Skokholm
Skomer
Slimbridge
Snettisham
Solway, WWB Caerlaverock
Southerness Point
South Foreland, Dover, Kent
Spey Mouth
Spey Valley, WWB Speyside
Spiggie, Loch, Shetland Mainland
Spurn Point, see Hot Spots
Staines Reservoir
Start Point
Steepholm
Stenness, Loch
Stodmarsh
Stoke Newington Reservoir
Stornoway Woods
Stour Estuary
Strathbeg, Loch of

Strath Polly (see WWB Inverpolly)
Sula Sgeir, WWB Berneray
Sule Skerry, WWB Berneray
Sule Stack, WWB Berneray
Summer Isles
Swale Estuary
Swanage, Dorset
Tamar Estuary
Tatton Park Mere
Tay Estuary
Teesmouth
Tentsmuir Point
Tewkesbury
Thames Estuary, Erith, Kent
Tiree
Titchfield
Torridge-Taw WWB Torridge Estuary
Torridon, WWB Beinn Eighe
Towy Valley, north of Carmarthen, Dyfed
Traeth Bach
Tregaron Bog
Tring Reservoirs
Troup Head
Uist, South, WWB Loch Druidibeg
Unst
Virginia Water
Walberswick, see Hot Spots
Walney Island
Walthamstow Reservoirs
Wash, The, WWB Holbeach, etc.
Weald, hills of Kent and Sussex
Weirwood Reservoir
Wells, see Hot Spots
Westray
Whipsnade, Luton, Hertfordshire
Wigtown Bay
William Girling Reservoir, Chingford, London
Windsor Great Park
Woburn, Bedfordshire
Wrath, Cape
Yare Marshes, WWB Breydon Water
Yell
Ythan Estuary

INDEX

This index includes only those species dealt with in the main body of the book and not in the section on rarities.